AS SEEN ON TV

Library of Congress Cataloging in Publication Number: 2002104029

ISBN: 1-931686-09-2

Printed in Singapore

Typeset in Futura, House Gothic, and Tiki Holiday.

Designed by Bryn Ashburn

Distributed in North America by Chronicle Books
85 Second Street
San Francisco, CA 94105

10 9 8 7 6 5 4 3 2 1

Quirk Books
215 Church Street
Philadelphia, PA 19106
www.quirkbooks.com

Photography credits

Ronco video stills courtesy of Edward Dormer, Philadelphia, Pennsylvania. All other photographs are copyright © 2002 www.photodrake.com except: pages 6 and 67 (Richard Simmons, Greenblatt/Getty Images), 16 (George Forman, Harvey/Getty), 64 (Susan Powter, Arroyo/Getty Images), 65 (Susan Powter, King/Getty Images), 74 (Burt Reynolds, Keeler/Getty Images; Pat Boone, Wolfson/Getty Images; Ricardo Montalbon, Jacobs/Getty Images; Susan Anton, Makos/Getty Images; Loni Anderson, Langdon/Getty Images), 86 (Charlton Heston, Shai/Getty Images), 92 (Dean Martin, Bob Hope, Sinatra, etc., Nairin/Getty Images), and page 17 and page 22 (courtesy of Salton, Inc.); pages 18–19 and Ginsu photo on page 6 (courtesy of Barry Becher & Ed Valenti); pages 24, 27, 43, and 141 (courtesy of Popeil Inventions, Inc.); pages 36–37 (courtesy of BluBlocker Corporation); page 40 (courtesy of Flowbee International); page 47 (courtesy of AP/World Wide Photos); page 51 (Turbie Twist photos courtesy of Smart Inventions, Inc.; Darla Haun photo courtesy of Darla Haun); page 56 (courtesy of Body by Jake Enterprises); pages 62–63 (courtesy of Icon Fitness); page 66 (© Mitchell Gerber/CORBIS); pages 70–71 (courtesy of Integrity Global Marketing); page 72 (courtesy of ThighMaster World Corporation); pages 84–85 (courtesy of Boxcar Willie Theater, Branson, MO); pages 88–89 and page 91 (courtesy of Joseph Enterprises, Inc.); pages 112–113 (courtesy of Garden Weasel Division/Faultless Starch/Bon Ami, CO, K.C., MO); pages 116–117 and Billy Mays photo on page 6 (courtesy of OrangeGlo International); pages 118–119 and Roto Zip photo on page 6 (courtesy of Roto Zip); pages 128–129 (courtesy of Matthew Lesko, Information USA, Inc.); pages 130–131 (courtesy of The Anthony Robbins Companies); page 142 (courtesy of Applica). Special thanks to David Duzenski, the model who appears on pages 55, 59, 60, 68, and 69.

AS SEEN ON TV

50 Amazing Products and the Commercials That Made Them Famous

BY LOU HARRY AND SAM STALL

QUIRK BOOKS
PHILADELPHIA

DEDICATION

This book is dedicated to my daughters, Emily (who gave me my first Flowbee haircut), Katie (who was the first to sample my homemade turkey jerky), and Maggie (Queen of Blopen art).

—Lou

I'm dedicating this one to my wife (and research assistant), Jami, who during the writing of this book found humor in everything from exploding microwave egg cookers to hyperactive Clappers.

—Sam

TABLE OF CONTENTS

introduction

Forget what George Orwell wrote. The most earth-shattering thing that happened in the year 1984 had nothing to do with global totalitarianism. Global marketing, maybe, but not global totalitarianism.

The really big change, the one that affects us even today, was that year's deregulation of the broadcast industry.

When the Federal Communications Commission loosened the reigns on how many ads broadcasters could air during a given hour of programming (and, more importantly, how long those ads could be), savvy marketers jumped into the fray. And guess what they brought us.

Educational fare? Nope.

Better service? Yeah, right.

Giant commercials? Yes, yes, and yes again. Overnight the traditional advertising spots were biggie-sized beyond all reason. Thirty seconds of pitch swelled into 30 minutes of kitsch. If these commercials were sold in stores, you'd have to buy them at Sam's Club—on a skid.

The only thing stranger than the humongous ads was the public's reaction to them. Did Americans rise up to reject this outrageous intrusion into their homes? Did the rank and file shout down the powers that be, stating in no uncertain terms that the promised land of 100 channels should not be clogged with 24-hour shopping; workout kings offering to tighten everything from your face to thighs; and come-ons for devices

that do everything from cook your dinner to make mountains of beef jerky?

Of course not. Quite the opposite, in fact. We actually found CTV (all commercials, all the time) kind of entertaining—in a half-asleep, nothing-else-on-at-2 A.M., can't-find-the-remote sort of way. The pitches, uninterrupted by annoying sitcoms, dramas, or other traditional television "programs," taught us things we didn't realize we needed to know. We were introduced to Billy Mays. And Billy Blanks. We Rotozipped planks and watched shirtless sorority skanks. We danced with Richard Simmons, grilled with George Foreman, and turned bags of vegetables into glasses of mouthwatering (or so it appeared) juice.

And as long as we had a credit card and telephone handy, we were never alone.

Of course the As Seen on TV (ASOTV) phenomenon was around long before 1984. The roots of the infomercial—as the new long-form ads are called—can be traced back to the glory days of the Ginsu and the remarkable ride of Ronco. Those founding fathers of direct-mail television advertising could say in 30 seconds what modern marketers need half an hour to explain.

Was it really their products that fascinated (and continue to fascinate) us, or was it the chutzpah behind

them? Let's face it: even though we might not need the latest ab-crunching device or labor-saving kitchen gadget, you've got to admire the sheer nerve of the promoters who think we do—and believe it so strongly that they'll buy millions of dollars of TV time to convince us.

In an age of multinational corporations, the ASOTV universe is still a place where a man with a semi-brilliant idea (say, a home rotisserie unit or an audio switch that turns things on and off when you clap) can, with some guts and brains and seed money, bring his product to market and become rich.

And if he could do it, why not us? We could test market our hot idea on a cable system outside Columbus, Ohio. If it sells there, then we'll take it to the Midwest. From there we go into heavy national rotation. Next thing you know, we're attending the Electronic

Retailers Association's annual convention, graciously accepting an Infomercial of the Year award from Marilu Henner or Judith Light. In short, tucked between the lines in every infomercial lives the very spirit of American entrepreneurship—and a resounding repudiation of the idea that there's nothing new under the sun.

What you'll see in the following pages is a celebration of both old-school ASOTV gadgets and today's infomercial stars. It's a guide to a merchandiser's Neverland where millions are made—and baldness can be cured with an aerosol can.

And best of all, you don't have to wait four to six weeks for delivery.

Clockwise from far left: the Roto Zip Spiral Saw; OxiClean pitchman Billy Mays; the legendary Ginsu Knives; GLH Formula #9; The Clapper; fitness guru Richard Simmons.

Before you immerse yourself in the wacky world of "operators are standing by" products, let's see how much you know about the goods that are sold through the tube.

1. WHICH OF THE FOLLOWING WAS A HIT SONG FOR SLIM WHITMAN?

a. "They Call the Wind Maria"
b. "Rose Marie"
c. "Along Comes Mary"

2. WHICH OF THE FOLLOWING IS NOT AN ENTRY IN THE DORF VIDEO SERIES?

a. *Dorf da Bingo King*
b. *Dorf Goes Fishing*
c. *Dorf Does Dallas*

3. JAY KORDICH IS ALSO KNOWN AS . . .

a. Mr. Microphone
b. The Juiceman
c. Billy Blopen

4. GINSU KNIVES ARE A PRODUCT OF . . .

a. Tokyo
b. Osaka
c. Ohio

5. *CHARLTON HESTON PRESENTS THE BIBLE* WAS PRODUCED BY HESTON'S . . .

a. Wife
b. Son
c. Bodyguard

6. BILLY MAYS IS . . .

a. The OxiClean guy
b. The As Seen on TV PC guy
c. The Bloussant guy

7. WHICH PRODUCT LAUNCHED THE IMMORTAL PHRASE "HELP! I'VE FALLEN AND I CAN'T GET UP!"?

a. LifeCall Alert System
b. Medalert
c. MediHelp

8. BOTH GLH FORMULA #9 AND NAD'S WERE ORIGINALLY DEVELOPED IN WHAT COUNTRY?

a. Greece
b. Australia
c. Brazil

9. WHICH OF THE FOLLOWING ITEMS IS AN ACTUAL PRODUCT SOLD BY THE FOLKS WHO MAKE DR-HO'S MUSCLE MASSAGE SYSTEM?

a. The Garden Ho
b. The Ho Fun Pillow
c. The Ho Lotta Shakin' Goin' On Massager

10. WHICH ONE OF THE FOLLOWING LINES DID RONCO FOUNDER RON POPEIL NEVER UTTER ON TV?

a. "Isn't that amazing!"
b. "It slices! It dices!"
c. "Makes mounds of julienned fries!"

11. THE LAST NAME OF THE MAN BEHIND BODY BY JAKE IS . . .

a. Steinberg
b. Seinfeld
c. Steinfeld

12. WHAT FIRM MARKETS THE GARDEN WEASEL?

a. The Faultless Starch/Bon Ami Company
b. Fingerhut
c. Ronco

13. WHAT OTHER FAMOUS ASOTV ITEM IS MARKETED BY THE SAME COMPANY THAT PRODUCES THE CHIA PET?

a. Blopens
b. Buttoneer
c. The Clapper

14. WHAT WAS LIQUID LEATHER ORIGINALLY CALLED?

a. Minute Mender
b. Leather Fixer
c. Gimme Some Skin

15. WHAT DOES THE GLH IN GLH FORMULA #9 STAND FOR?

a. Gals Love Hair
b. Grow Lotsa Hair
c. Great Looking Hair

SCORING

Give yourself one point for each correct answer.

POINTS	WHAT YOUR SCORE MEANS
0–3	Welcome back from the retreat, Mr. Monk. You can talk now.
4–8	You may have noticed this magic box in your living room. It's called a TV.
9–12	You probably own a George Foreman Grill, OxiClean, or other products that actually work.
13–15	You are an insomniac with too many credit cards.

QUIZ ANSWERS

1. (b) "Rose Marie"
2. (c) *Dorf Does Dallas*
3. (b) The Juiceman
4. (c) Ohio
5. (b) Son
6. (a) The OxiClean guy
7. (c) LifeCall Alert System
8. (b) Australia
9. (b) The Ho Fun Pillow
10. (b) "It slices! It dices!"
11. (c) Steinfeld
12. (a) The Faultless Starch/Bon Ami Company
13. (c) The Clapper
14. (a) Minute Mender
15. (c) Great Looking Hair

part 1

KITCHEN MARVELS

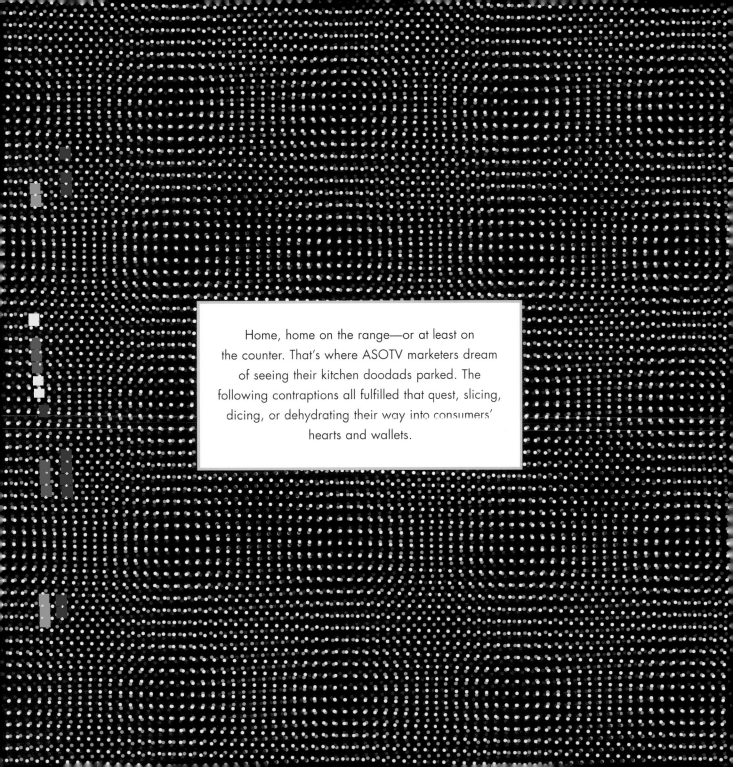

Home, home on the range—or at least on the counter. That's where ASOTV marketers dream of seeing their kitchen doodads parked. The following contraptions all fulfilled that quest, slicing, dicing, or dehydrating their way into consumers' hearts and wallets.

veg-o-matic

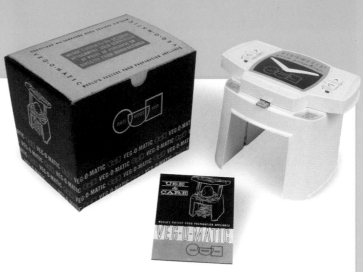

"Isn't that amazing?!?"

For Edison it was the lightbulb. For Ford it was the Model T. For Ron Popeil, the king of ASOTV products, it was a once-ubiquitous kitchen gadget called the Veg-O-Matic. Every brilliant innovator, you see, has one creation that tips him into greatness.

Okay, so Ron Popeil didn't actually create this particular wonder (as he would later do with a jaw-dropping array of items, from the Inside the Shell Egg Scrambler to the Showtime Rotisserie & BBQ). The achievement belongs to his father, Samuel Jacob (S. J.) Popeil, an inventor/marketer in his own right who trotted out an entire line of "O-Matic" machines. There was the Chop-O-Matic (a canister-shaped affair that allowed the user to chop produce by pounding on a piston-like attachment hooked to an array of blades); the Dial-O-Matic (a veggie slicer whose cutting thickness could be changed via its namesake dial); and his crowning achievement, the Veg-O-Matic.

That contraption, which debuted in the early '60s, was basically a hand-powered food processor. Just place a vegetable on a platform over the cutting blades (which could be adjusted to slice, dice, or wedge) and push down. Nowadays this doesn't seem like such a big deal, but in the pre-food processor era, plowing through mountains of produce without

THE PRODUCT

A vegetable processing device that used two sets of rotating blades to slice, dice, or chop.

STATUS: Off the market.

CLAIMED INNOVATION: It sliced super quick.

THE UPSIDE: It really was fast. According to company calculations, it could create 1,150 shoestring fries in a minute.

THE DOWNSIDE: It required considerable hand strength to be used efficiently. Ron Popeil is said to possess a viselike grip earned from years of demonstrating the various members of the O-Matic family.

breaking a sweat (or slicing open a finger) was considered quite an achievement—and well worth the $7.77 required to obtain it.

The spiel for the original ad is so brief it can be recited in one breath—as Popeil, who did the narration like an auctioneer on speed, ably demonstrated. Nevertheless it was effective enough to sell some 11 million units. Demand was so great that customers actually got into Cabbage Patch Kids–style brawls at stores when supplies ran short.

Unfortunately the Veg-O-Matic was driven from the market when electric food processors made it even easier to slice, dice, and julienne. It lives on in memory—though sometimes that memory is a bit murky. Genre fans may swear to have heard Ron Popeil say, "It slices! It dices!" but he insists he never uttered this famous catchphrase. And he's got the videotape to prove it.

HOW it GOt ON TV

Popeil spent his formative years selling his father's kitchen doodads and other trinkets at the nation's flagship Woolworth's store in Chicago—back in the glory days when five-and-dimes had flagship stores. Even though he made $1,000 a week (circa 1955, that was a very, very nice paycheck), he couldn't help thinking there was a better way. What if he could make his pitch in front of thousands at a time instead of dozens? Then he wouldn't have to sell his wares from dawn to dusk, shouting himself hoarse every day.

He found what he needed in television.

Popeil made his first TV spot for a little something called the Ronco Spray Gun. It could do anything from wash a car to fertilize a lawn, depending on which of several types of dissolving pellets were inserted into its spray chamber (make a mistake and you got either a very soapy lawn or an insect-free auto). That first spot cost $550, with Popeil using a buddy's car for the demonstration and doing the voice work himself. Nevertheless it helped move almost 1 million units within four years. Ron's father, S. J., was suitably impressed. He asked his son to market the Chop-O-Matic the same way, and then the Veg-O-Matic. The rest is boob tube history.

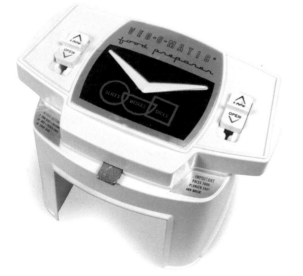

Egg Wave

"Have an eggstraordinary day!"

Every generation, it seems, faces some overwhelming technical problem that challenges its greatest minds. During World War II it was the development of the atomic bomb. During the '60s it was the exploration of outer space. These days it's the struggle to prepare delicious (or at least edible) eggs in the shortest possible time. The Egg Wave is perhaps the crowning achievement of this culinary arms race.

It certainly sports the most appealing design. The unit consists of four egg-shaped containers positioned on an Egg Caddy for easy transport. Want an egg sunny-side up? Just crack one into a container, nuke it for 30 seconds, extract it with the handy-dandy Egg Remover, and enjoy a soft-yolk breakfast. If you want it scrambled, insert the gridded Egg Scrambler into one (or more) of the pods, drop in an egg, shake vigorously, and then zap it for 45 seconds. The unit can cook four eggs at a time, one in each pod.

Unfortunately the final product isn't nearly as aesthetically pleasing as the device that creates it. Conventional eggs look like the ones plopped inside McDonald's Egg McMuffins, while the scrambled versions are yellowish, puck-like things that would disturb even a high school cafeteria worker. Given the final product's funky appearance, one could almost forgive

THE PRODUCT

Four microwavable egg-shaped pods, each of which can hold one egg.

STATUS: On the market.

CLAIMED INNOVATION: Cooks eggs quickly in the microwave.

THE UPSIDE: It cooks 'em, all right.

THE DOWNSIDE: Cook them too little and they come out runny. Cook them too much and they turn putrid shades of green and gray.

Caveat

If you forget to close the vent on top of the pods before shaking them to make scrambled eggs, you'll coat your walls with uncooked yolk. And if you forget to open the vent before cooking, the container will explode.

the Egg Wave folks if, for their commercials and print ads, they took a little artistic license and fanned out the scrambled eggs with a fork. But instead they're for the most part presented *au naturel*, some even decked with viscous, phlegm-like sauce.

It's easy to understand why chefs consider microwaved eggs to be a culinary atrocity on par with boiled beef. The manufacturer seems to acknowledge this problem in the little recipe booklet accompanying each unit. The lineup of "treats" includes several sauces to pour over the eggs so that presumably you won't have to look at them while you dine.

WHO'S BEHIND IT?

Thank the folks at TriStar Products, a direct marketing firm with a massive lineup of ASOTV goods. The list includes such wonders as the ABSculptor (you can't be a direct marketer without at least one stomach-flattening gizmo), Banjo Lure Fishing System, Eurosealer, Contour Cloud Pillow, Shoe Tree Carousel, Steam Buggy (see page 120), Tap Teaser, Hook 'N Hang, Turbo Tiger, and Hairflex. We have no idea what the last four products do, but we love the names.

THE NEXT WAVE

Inventors and marketers seem fascinated by microwaved eggs. How else to explain the multiple products designed to accomplish this? The Egg Wave's leading ASOTV competitor is the Perfect Omelet. It's hawked by a cheerful fellow with the unfortunate name of Mick Hastie, who clearly assumes that his audience lacks basic motor skills. "Have you ever tried to flip an omelet?" he asks. "It's near impossible." The alternative? Pour two beaten eggs into each side of the Perfect Omelet, throw on whatever else you want, nuke, mix a bit, nuke again, then flip the two pulsating mounds together for one final dose of radiation. The result is far from perfect, but it does taste somewhat like an omelet. Plus, cleanup is far easier than with the Egg Wave.

GEORGE FOREMAN'S
Lean Mean Fat-Reducing
GRILLING MACHINE

"Knock out the fat!"

One of the greatest heavyweight linkups since *Frankenstein Meets the Wolfman* occurred in 1993 when the marketing firm Salton Inc. trotted out a new line of tabletop grills designed for low-fat cooking. Although this was hardly an earthshaking concept, the otherwise ho-hum device had two things going for it: a great name (The Lean Mean Fat-Reducing Grilling Machine) and a high-level celebrity endorser—smiling, chrome-domed boxer-turned-pitchman George Foreman.

At first glance the Olympic gold medalist and former heavyweight champion seems a lousy choice for appliance sales. There was certainly nothing Ron Popeil-ish about his boxing career, where his reputation as a coldhearted gladiator intimidated even the most seasoned fighters. But then in 1977 Foreman underwent a religious conversion and became a preacher. Perhaps all those Sundays spent praising the Lord also taught him how to praise products.

He got plenty of experience when he staged a boxing comeback and, against all odds, briefly regained the championship in 1994 at the age of 45. Soon a long

THE PRODUCT

A clamshell grill that cooks food on both sides at the same time. A slight incline allows excess grease to drain into a catch tray.

STATUS: On the market.

CLAIMED INNOVATION: Convenient low-fat cooking.

THE UPSIDE: Cooks meat in no time flat.

THE DOWNSIDE: The grill gets hotter the longer it's used, meaning that while your first burger may be cooked to perfection, your fourth may turn into a hockey puck in the same amount of time.

UNAUTHORIZED USE

One word: S'mores. Sure the marshmallows don't get golden brown, but the whole package (provided you time it exactly right) does emerge hot and melty. Just don't crush the graham crackers or allow the chocolate and/or marshmallow to run.

list of deep-pocketed corporations, including Nike and McDonald's, lined up to get the highly bankable Foreman in their corner. But he saved his tour de force for the grilling machine spots, which are still broadcast nationwide. As he banters with the infomercial hosts, an apron wrapped around his prodigious gut, Foreman radiates an easygoing, I'm-just-happy-to-be-here attitude that's as far from his old ring persona as a preacher is from a pugilist.

His genial presence helped sell more than 10 million grills and ignite an almost cultlike enthusiasm for the product. Few people would admit to owning, say, an Egg Wave or Great American Steakhouse Onion Machine, yet Foreman fans proudly boast of using their machines daily. Even New York City's Tavern on the Green restaurant professes to keeping them handy.

But although Foreman greatly expanded his fame and fortune by endorsing this fat-fighting contraption, his own appetite is unabashedly voracious. The former champ is famous for his love of high-fat chow. His church bus is even nicknamed the "Cheez Burger Express."

caveat

"It shouldn't be thought of as something that makes foods lower in fat than other grills—all grills, after all, drain fat. But the ridged, nonstick surface does indeed do the job, which is what accounts for the 'lean mean fat-reducing machine' moniker. Foreman grill fans should keep in mind that low-fat grilling doesn't mean you can eat like a heavyweight boxer. A sensible serving of meat is 3 ounces, regardless of what machine it's cooked on."

—Tufts University Health & Nutrition Letter

POP Question

HOW LONG DOES IT TAKE TO COOK STUFF?

You can cook a T-bone to rare in eight minutes; a salmon fillet to well done in four and a half minutes; and pork chops to well done in 17 minutes. Interestingly, the instructions also note cooking times for "rare" chops. That's nine minutes for you trichinosis fans.

Ginsu Knives

"Now how much would you pay?"

Knives are a staple on the product demonstration circuit. Any pitchman worth his spiel cuts his teeth (not to mention his cucumbers, his shoe, and, if he's not careful, his fingers) proving that his blades are better than whatever currently resides in his audience's kitchens. Can *their* knives cut a tomato this thin? Of course not. And before the typical customer can think too deeply about why *anyone* would want such thin tomatoes, he's bought a set and received a free paring knife for his trouble.

Why is cutlery such an easy sell? For one thing, everybody needs it. For another, most people haven't a clue what a quality blade should cost. And finally, it's easy to throw in extras (such as the aforementioned paring knife) to sweeten the deal. Those advantages make them perfect for television marketing. But even with so much in their favor, who could have predicted that a simple set of knives was destined to become an ASOTV legend?

Apparently no one save for ad salesman Ed Valenti and AAMCO Transmission entrepreneur Barry Becher. These marketing masters were the brains behind a grab bag of products,

THE PRODUCT

Knives. Really sharp knives.

STATUS: On the market.

CLAIMED INNOVATION: Able to cut things kitchen cutlery is rarely called upon to cut.

THE UPSIDE: No-brainer wedding gift.

THE DOWNSIDE: You can get similar quality at Target.

Cutting-Edge Humor

With the possible exception of the ThighMaster, Ginsus are the most laughed-about product in the ASOTV menagerie. Homages stretch from cartoons in *The New Yorker* to the monologues of late-night talk show hosts. Alas, like much of America, David Letterman's Top 10 List once mistakenly credited them to Ronco.

such as Claudete Louberge Hosiery, Royal Durasteel, The "Chainge" Adjustable Necklace, and Armourcote Cookware. But their special blade wouldn't be marketed in-person by pitchmen. It had to make its case on TV, during lightning-quick 30-second spots. To accomplish this the duo produced commercials that cut to the chase quicker than a Ginsu could slice through a tin can.

The men filled their commercials with rapid-fire images of the knives in action, dismembering everything from produce to nails. Over these visuals flowed innovative phrases that for all intents and purposes pioneered the lexicon of all ASOTV ads to come. "But wait, there's more," viewers were told. Then they were asked, "Now how much would you pay?" and were advised to "Act now and you'll also receive . . ." Sure they're clichés now, but to virginal television audiences they were newly minted, masterfully delivered seduction lines.

Apparently they still have the power to charm. After more than $50 million in sales, Ginsu Knives are still proving themselves, one tomato at a time.

POP QUESTION

WHAT DOES "GINSU" MEAN?

Is it the name of a famous Samurai? The moniker of an ancient cutlery manufacturer? Dream on. Ginsu means nothing—not in Japanese, not in English. In fact, the closest Japanese-sounding word we could locate is *ginsunago*, which translates as "silver dust." The legendary blades are, however, a product of the East—the eastern United States, that is. Specifically, Freemont, Ohio, home to the Quikut Division of Scott & Fetzer.

Ginsu guys Barry Becher (above) and Ed Valenti (right) on the set of a commercial.

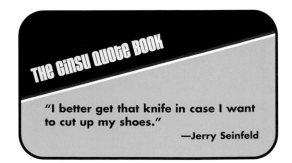

THE GINSU QUOTE BOOK

"I better get that knife in case I want to cut up my shoes."
—Jerry Seinfeld

BUYING INTO THE BIG LEAGUES

At one time Valenti and Becher were the 18th-largest buyers of spot television time in America, sandwiched between Coca-Cola and AT&T.

THE Great Wok of China

"The same one used in China!"

You've got to admire the folks who created The Great Wok of China. Not for their originality or daring—they were sorely lacking in both—but for their chutzpah. It takes a great deal of nerve to take a widely known, widely available product, build a marketing campaign around it, and then call it the Next Big Thing. It's as if Ron Popeil came out with the Ronco Toothpick.

But that's essentially what the Great Wok folks did—took a cooking tool as old as time and converted it into a marketing phenomenon.

The Great Wok of China, one of television's earliest direct-response hits, didn't improve on a basic product. Nor did it offer a radical variation. It didn't even simplify a complex procedure. Instead, it merely introduced the product to a new audience.

Like many of its infomercial brethren, the Great Wok spent years on the fair circuit before the infomercial boom hit. The ancient cooking device was ideally suited to this latest television marketing trick, because you could cook an entire wok meal in 18 minutes. That left plenty of time for endorsements, special

THE PRODUCT

A hand-hammered, 14-inch steel wok with an "ultra-flat mini-bottom."

STATUS: On the market.

CLAIMED INNOVATION: Low-fat cooking the Asian way.

THE UPSIDE: Woks are great cooking tools.

THE DOWNSIDE: Woks are available absolutely everywhere. Have a wedding shower and you'll get four.

offers, the posting of 1–800 numbers, the pitching of money-back guarantees if you weren't completely satisfied, etc.

The makers of the Great Wok ads never bothered with celebrity plugs (unless you count recent infomercial appearances by a guy named Chef Richard). Instead, the original ad featured veteran pitchman Wally Nash. The ads were simple—basically a televised version of the in-person demonstration you can see at your local home show—but they struck a chord. Even its marketers are somewhat at a loss to explain it. "With any direct response," says Max Ker-Seymer, president of Westminster Inc., which now offers the Great Wok, "you throw it on the air and see if it sells. Sometimes they catch people's imagination. You get a brand that comes out of nowhere, one that has some magic."

our Favorite wok Joke

Quasimodo comes home from work and finds that his mother has the wok out.

"Oh no," says the hunchback. "I hate Chinese food."

"Relax," says his mother. "I'm just ironing your shirts."

POP Question

WHAT'S A WOK?

Basically it's just a frying pan shaped like a bowl. Developed thousands of years ago in China, it began life as a cast-iron pan. The curved surface concentrates heat on the bottom, allowing food to be cooked quickly with minimal fuel. In American homes, it's used two or three times, then put up on a high shelf.

THE Juiceman Automatic Juice Extractor

"It's the juice of the fiber that feeds you."

Even in the overheated, hard-sell world of TV pitchpeople, The Juiceman is in his own, special world. His own special, wild-eyed, evangelical, borderline-scary world.

Clad in the international uniform of the health conscious (sneakers and a jogging outfit) and sporting Einstein-like eyebrows that seem to arrive a couple of minutes before the rest of him does, The Juiceman (real name: Jay Kordich) relentlessly, passionately trumpets the life-giving pleasures of a beverage most humans haven't thought much about since grade school: juice.

Not just any juice, mind you, but liquid that's consumed just moments after it's ripped from the flesh of fruits or vegetables. This is apparently quite important, because if you let juice sit around, its healthful properties can dissipate as quickly as a sno-cone on a hot sidewalk. "As soon as the fiber surrounding the juice is broken open in the juicing process, the oxidation process begins," sayeth The Juiceman. "All of the enzymes and food value contained in the fresh juice are most beneficial immediately after juicing."

THE PRODUCT

Centrifugal machine that separates liquid from pulp by spinning it over sharp blades. Juice comes out one end, pulp emerges from the other.

STATUS: On the market.

CLAIMED INNOVATION: You can grind the skin of a watermelon or pineapple without damaging the motor.

THE UPSIDE: If you believe the "Juice Is Life" credo, then this device can add decades to your existence.

THE DOWNSIDE: Every tasty or semi-tasty concoction you whip up leaves behind a mound of sticky bilge.

UNAUTHORIZED USE

Many of the juice combinations benefit greatly from a splash of vodka.

Zoiks. Given this breathtakingly short half-life, we'd be fools to trust our juice needs to the folks at Minute Maid. Instead, the pope of pulp says we must make it ourselves, preferably using the food processor-sized system he pitches (which is also known as The Juiceman). "This is something you don't buy as a whim, as a gadget," The Juiceman insists during one of his many infomercials. "I mean, this is the blood of your body."

But that's, as they say, not all. The Juiceman has been credited not only with selling his own machine (the original cost: $289), but also with putting a positive spin on the entire juicer industry. For manufacturers with a stake in this business, Kordich is their greatest liquid asset.

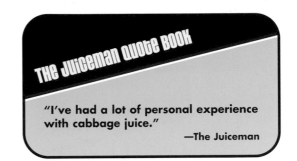
POP QUESTION

WHY DOES IT HAVE TO BE JUICE?

Because folks would find it a little too time consuming—not to mention filling—to eat the massive amounts of vegetables and fruit The Juiceman advocates (for instance, it takes four cups of raw carrots to make a cup of carrot juice). Plus, in liquid form, the good stuff makes a beeline for the bloodstream.

SPIN-OFFS

The Juiceman's Power of Juicing (William Morrow & Company) hit the *New York Times* best-seller list and sold more than half a million hard-cover copies.

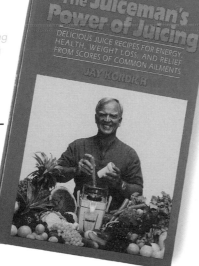

THE JUICEMAN COMETH

Though the value of consuming gallons of liquified carrots/beets/celery/[insert favorite vegetable here] can be debated, the single-minded devotion of The Juiceman (Kordich) can't. A veteran of the county fair circuit, he's extolled the virtues of juicing for more than 50 years—ever since, shortly after being drafted by the Green Bay Packers, he discovered he had bladder cancer. Unhappy with the usual treatment prescribed for the disease at that time (namely, get your affairs in order), he got in touch with a doc who treated patients with juice and other natural foods. Moving from California to New York to be near his beverage guru, he went on a diet of carrot-apple juice and calf liver. And so, he says, he's been in remission ever since.

RONCO ELECTRIC FOOD DEHYDRATOR
and yogurt maker and Beef jerky machine

"Save hundreds of dollars by doing it yourself."

A *Saturday Night Live* mock commercial once touted a product that was both a floor wax and a dessert topping. The humor, of course, sprang from the fact that these two radically different needs couldn't possibly be served by a single item. Yet is that combination any stranger than a real-life machine that could make both beef jerky and yogurt? Indeed, this device could do that and more. It turned meat into jerky, milk into yogurt, and the formerly washed-up Ron Popeil into a hot commodity.

In the mid- to late 1980s it would have been easy to write off Popeil. The king of the ASOTV universe was in semiretirement, his legendary company, Ronco, a Chapter 11 casualty. The Salad Spinner, Mr. Microphone (see page 102), and the Veg-O-Matic (see page 12) were distant memories.

Nevertheless, Popeil decided to sally forth for another swing at fame and fortune, and entered an advertising

THE PRODUCT

A machine that heats food to drain its moisture.

STATUS: On the market.

CLAIMED INNOVATION: Health food (except for the jerky) from a made-in-the-USA machine.

THE UPSIDE: It makes banana chips for less than you'd spend at the health food store.

THE DOWNSIDE: Banana chips suck.

UNAUTHORIZED USE

Excellent way to preserve Play-Doh sculptures.

world very different from the one he'd left. The 30-second spot was no longer the driving force for electronic retailing, and QVC and the Home Shopping Network were redefining the "call now" landscape. But Popeil adapted. He hooked up with a satellite TV shopping show and sold 232 units on his first day in front of a camera.

Units of what? A food dehydrator, of all things. Afterward, Popeil made his own infomercial for the beehive-shaped device, scriptless and serving as his own on-screen talent. Watching the great one's resurgence was like witnessing Michael Jordan's return to the NBA—only Popeil still had all his moves.

One could argue that he was better than ever. After all, this time he wasn't hawking some "useful" item that reduced the drudgery of kitchen work. This product actually created drudgery. It also ate up counter space and, priced at $60 in 1991 money, was far from an impulse buy.

And yet, Popeil managed to sell hundreds of thousands of units. Maybe there was a vast, untapped market for dried meat out there. Or maybe, just maybe, infomercial fans succumbed to a salesman so skilled he could make food dehydrators sound appealing. After this, what could possibly challenge Popeil? Perhaps selling snow to Eskimos—or space heaters to the Devil.

SPREADING CULTURE

To make yogurt in the food dehydrator, start with a cup of milk . . . and store-bought yogurt. Two tablespoons must be added for every cup of moo juice.

No book about television's greatest inventions would be complete without a few words from the man who started it all, Ronco founder Ron Popeil. When we reached him at his Beverly Hills home, the master of the ASOTV universe was doing pretty much what he always does—tinkering with new inventions in one of his two (yes, two) commercial kitchens. He keeps a complete office with dozens of employees just a few miles down the road, but as the man who marketed everything from the Ronco Smokeless Ashtray to Mr. Microphone readily admits, this is where the real work gets done. We couldn't resist running some semi-serious questions past the father of TV direct marketing.

WHAT ARE YOU DOING RIGHT THIS SECOND?

I was just pulling a 24-pound turkey out of the restaurant model of my Showtime Rotisserie. It's only 50 percent larger from left to right than the original, but it does a 24-pound turkey. It also does four chickens at once. Four-chicken commercial rotisseries sell for between $6,000 and $8,000. I'll be able to sell this for $499.

ISN'T THAT AMAZING! DO YOU GET RECOGNIZED ON THE STREET?

People come up and say hello to me. My daughter will ask, "Do you know that person?" and I'll say, "No." But when you spend the kind of money that I do to put your face on television, and you have a product people like, your name and face are going to be remembered.

WHAT DO PEOPLE ASK YOU?

It's not a question. Normally it's a statement, referring to one of my products and how much they love it and can't do without it. Or they'll look at me and say, "Hey Ron, set it and forget it!" That's a big thing. And when I had Mr. Microphone many years ago, they'd look at me and say, "Hey good lookin', I'll be back to pick you up later!"

WHAT'S THE BIGGEST MISTAKE AN INFOMERCIAL MAKER CAN COMMIT?

Going after an audience that's too small because they've created a product that's not generic enough to appeal to most viewers. Say it appeals to people who make model airplanes. How could anybody go after an audience that small? I go after everyone who's got a kitchen. The product I select has gigantic appeal, because it has to stand the cost of the media.

WHAT'S THE OTHER BIGGEST MISTAKE?

Ninety-five percent of the people who come into the infomercial business lose their shirts, because the cost of buying television time can bury you. Say you come into this business with a product, maybe a kitchen item, that meets the criteria of mass marketing. Now you have to buy TV time. But how much are you going to pay for a noon slot on KTLA here in Los Angeles on a Sunday? You have to know, because anytime you walk into a business deal and you're at the mercy of someone who makes a commission based on the price they give you, you're dead in the water.

What makes the infomercial business work is this: Say you buy a spot at one o'clock on a Sunday afternoon on KTLA and you get 46 orders. Forget what you spent on the TV time. What matters is how many units you sold. If you buy that same slot next week or the week after that or the week after that, you'll always get around 46 orders. Now you can quantify what that slot is really worth to you. If you don't want to pay more than a dollar per unit for TV time, then you can't give the station more than 46 bucks. That's how we know when to tell a station, "Your price is too high. We only sold XX number of pieces when we ran it. This is all we can afford to pay."

WHICH OLD SCHOOL RONCO DEVICE DO YOU STILL USE?

I have an Inside the Shell Egg Scrambler that I use frequently. Of course that product would never rate an infomercial because it's too isolated and specialized. It was good in the old days, but in today's infomercial business it couldn't stand the cost of the media.

DON'T YOU ALSO STILL OFFER THE DIAL-O-MATIC?

The Dial-O-Matic is an inexpensive food slicer that was manufactured by my father. I was the one who developed the marketing on it. From time to time we still include it with new products. We included it with the Ronco Food Dehydrator, and we sold a million of

those in 1992. I made 19 million bucks off of the dehydrator in 1992, and an awful lot of them went out the door with a Dial-O-Matic included.

WHY DON'T YOU OFFER LITTLE THINGS LIKE THE SMOKELESS ASHTRAY ANYMORE?

I have a little project that I'm working on—a device that takes the place of a spatula. It's called the Flipper. I think everyone who ever cooked would like to have one of these. When I see this thing I just freak out. Unfortunately, I may make $4 or $5 million with this little gadget. That sounds like a lot of money, but unfortunately not to me. Maybe I'm a little callous. When you're used to making hundreds of millions of dollars and you have a chance to make $5 million on a project, you have to ask, "Is it worth my time?" If it's priced at $20 each, you can sell a jillion of them and not make that much. However, they make great giveaways with other products. I would not be a bit surprised if I threw one of these things in as a gift with my new pizza thing, which I'm working on now.

PIZZA THING? WHAT PIZZA THING?

Right now I can cook frozen pizzas so that they taste as good as homemade or delivery. I wanted to create (and I think I have) a product that's small in size but will do at least a 16-inch pizza and maybe an 18-inch pizza but not take up a lot of space. If that pizza is frozen—frozen—you will be eating it in 10 minutes. And it's crispy and hot and tastes fabulous. It also does a variety of other things. It will do frozen hash browns and frozen french fries. It will even toast a bunch of bagels at once. But when the infomercial for this product is made, 95 percent of the time will be devoted to the pizzas and 5 percent to the ancillary stuff. Someone else might devote 50 percent to pizzas and 50 percent to other things, but that's the wrong approach. If a product does too many things, you rob it of focus and that won't be good.

HOW DO YOU MAKE AN INFOMERCIAL?
Mine are 100 percent unscripted, which presents a series of problems. I've used seven cameramen and next time I'll probably use eight. I can never get enough because they never know where I'm going. I don't even know the hostess [who helps emcee the show], so she has to play off me without knowing what I'm going to do.

The one thing I do know is that for two or three weeks prior to taping she's had an opportunity to use the machine we're selling. The audience of 160 to 170 people has also had the chance to use the machine for two or three weeks. So although I don't know the audience members, they have used the machine and what they say about it is real.

HOW MANY TAKES DO YOU NEED TO GET AN INFOMERCIAL RIGHT?
Usually it's done in one take. The whole infomercial has to be shot in a day. You don't want to have overtime with the cameramen and equipment and other stuff you're renting.

IS THIS THE BEST PART OF YOUR CAREER RIGHT NOW?
Absolutely. The harder I work, the luckier I get. I've put in an awful lot of time, but I really enjoy what I'm doing. I never go to the [main administrative] office in Chatsworth. It's about 40 minutes from where I live in Beverly Hills. I hate going there because it's just one problem after another.

SO YOUR KITCHEN IS THE REAL RONCO COMMAND CENTER?
Yes, my two kitchens are in command. One guy [Popeil] makes all the decisions, which is hard to come by in most companies today. People say, "When you come up with an idea for a product, do you solicit opinions and feedback from a bunch of people?" I am the feedback. I test it. I'll tell you whether they're going to like it. I'll tell you what the problems are and how to solve them, if they are solvable. I am the audience.

DO INFOMERCIAL WANNA-BES OFTEN COME TO YOU FOR ADVICE?
All the time. And I try to give it to them all the time.

DO THEY LISTEN?
Everybody listens to me. I'm not patting myself on the back, but I've got close to 50 years in this business, and I'm the most successful at it in the world. Why wouldn't you listen to the guy who's the most successful at this in the world—and who's not charging you?

part 2

fashion & Beauty
wonders

Life would be so much easier if we only had more hair. Or less hair. Or bigger boobs. Or more rhinestones on our clothing. Fortunately, everything we need to make us more attractive (or at the very least, more distinctive) is just a commercial away.

BEDAZZLER

"Change everyday clothing into exciting fashions!"

Most ASOTV products enjoy a mayfly-brief moment of fame before disappearing into a ghostly afterworld of eBay postings and garage sales. Some may stay on the market for decades, some for mere months. Eventually, however, all must face that fateful day when operators are no longer standing by.

All except for a handful of products that, not unlike Aerosmith, manage to go from hot to lame to hot again. Such is the case with the BeDazzler (a.k.a. The Rhinestone and Stud Setter by Ronco). Originally marketed as a follow-up to Ronco's Bottle and Jar Cutter (the company was on a "craft" kick), the odd little device was created by Herman Brickman, a New England inventor whom Ronco boss Ron Popeil had previously tapped to help with the Bottle Cutter.

While a stud setter may sound like a dog breeding term, it's actually a device that looks like a toy sewing machine. With it, would-be rhinestone cowgirls can dude up their denim, perk up their purses, and tart up their tube tops. Simply choose the stud you want to use, insert it into the arm of the BeDazzler, turn the dial on the base to the proper

THE PRODUCT

A plastic device that attaches decorative elements to clothing.

STATUS: On the market.

CLAIMED INNOVATION: Easy to do and washable.

THE UPSIDE: You can turn tacky old clothes into rhinestoned extravaganzas.

THE DOWNSIDE: The clothes are still tacky, but in a more flamboyant way.

UNAUTHORIZED USE

Turn old flip-flops into tap shoes.

setting, and push down. Believe it or not, it actually stays on the garment.

But like any fashion trend, that first stud craze rode a steep, short bell curve from hot to not. Popeil admits that during its salad days he made a very unRonco-like faux pas—failing to secure the tooling rights for the machine. As a result, when Popeil moved on, inventor Brickman reintroduced the product under a new (and much catchier) name—BeDazzler. Offered to new generations without the slightest reference to its old Ronco pedigree, BeDazzler took the market by storm. Packaged both as a serious tool for crafty designers and as a kid's toy, it proved to be a marketing stud.

Star-Studded

Watch almost any award show from the first 18 months of the new century and you'll see celebs sporting glittery garb that could have come straight from the Liberace Museum gift shop. The BeDazzler was also featured in the premier issue of *Rosie* magazine. Even Monica Lewinsky, who knows a thing or two about handling studs, confessed in a *New York* magazine article to employing it.

THE BeDAZZLER QUOTE BOOK

"[Britney Spears] performed in a hot pink jumpsuit, which, while staying true to her 'no more cleavage' rule, made her look more like someone who had attacked a pink Gumby with the BeDazzler."

—freelance writer Julia Donahue, writing about the Grammy Awards on snowball.com

Bloussant

"Let's face it, ladies, not all of us are satisfied with our small bust size."

Peruse the back of almost any women's magazine and you'll find page after page of ads showing amply endowed women plugging products with names such as Bust Plus, Endow Plus, New Bust, Grobust, and even Wonderbreast. All are pills or creams that claim to increase bust size.

How does Bloussant stand out?

Simple. Bloussant has perky television ads featuring anatomically gifted women wafting across the screen, all filmed in the same soft focus used in Elizabeth Taylor's White Diamonds commercials. As vaguely sensual music trills in the background, a spokeswoman offers a sentence that sums up both this specific product and the guiding belief behind the entire market segment. "Let's face it ladies," she says. "Not all of us are satisfied with our small bust size."

Apparently not. Bloussant's approach seems to hinge on the assumption that lots of women, regardless of their life accomplishments, still stare wistfully into mirrors and think, "Damn, I could never be a Hooters waitress." And since nothing, apparently, boosts a lady's confidence and peace of mind quite like a

THE PRODUCT

Pills filled with herbs that allegedly promote the growth of breast tissue.

STATUS: On the market.

CLAIMED INNOVATION: Bigger breasts without surgery.

THE UPSIDE: If it works, fantastic. The guy who develops a similar pill for the male member will become richer than Bill Gates.

THE DOWNSIDE: Incredibly expensive, and you won't see results for weeks (if ever).

bodacious set of ta-tas, Bloussant offers to deliver them. In pill form.

So why aren't despairing plastic surgeons shaking in their Prada shoes over the prospect of big boobs in a bottle? Perhaps because Bloussant and its sister products are quite expensive. A 12-month supply costs a breathtaking $804.95. If you had to take the pills forever, breast augmentation surgery might actually be a better deal in the long run.

Bloussant and its competitors can count on innate human optimism to move product—particularly among the millions of women with A and B cups who watch the tube and think, "But what if it *did* work?" It's the same sort of desperation-fueled "logic" that's sold endless cases of GLH Formula #9 (see page 42) to balding men.

(see page 42)

POP QUESTION

HOW CAN A PILL OVERRIDE ONE'S GENETIC DESTINY?

The science behind Bloussant (and all other such products) is pretty sketchy, but here's the general theory. Each tablet contains a veritable spice rack of rack-building spices. The pharmacopoeia includes fennel seed, don quai, damiana, blessed thistle, black cohosh and many, many more. These compounds allegedly excite the female body into producing more progesterone, estrogen, prolactin and, most importantly, "growth factor hormones." For some not-very-well-explained reason, these supercharged hormones make a beeline for the bustline, where they have roughly the same effect that yeast has on dough. The Bloussant commercials illustrate this phenomenon with a computer simulation showing massive breasts instantaneously heaving up from a flat female torso. It's like a time-lapse view of the birth of the Rockies.

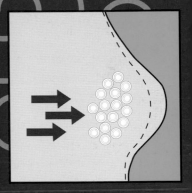

REASON TO LOCK UP YOUR DAUGHTERS

Seventeen magazine and *Teen Vogue* have both carried ads for Bloussant. Showing a bra-clad woman from the lips down, these print versions of the infomercial pitch promised their young readers "no more artificial padding or expensive surgical implants." When called on it (through Bloussant's 800 number, of course), a spokesperson insisted that the product is safe for anyone out of puberty and that they don't sell to anyone younger than 17.

SPIN-OFFS

Wellquest offers a full line of pills and salves addressing problems that most people probably don't consider fixable via pills and salves. There's Dsnore (an anti-snoring spray), Stretchaway (gets rid of stretch marks), and the horrifically named Veinish (it apparently does something to spider veins).

THE BLOUSSANT QUOTE BOOK

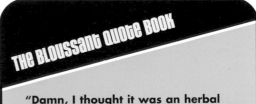

"Damn, I thought it was an herbal vitamin . . . but I will admit that I am looking rather sexy, my breasts are firmer, and I'm getting many hours of enjoyment."
— "Mark" in the www.overclocked.com chat room

BLUBLOCKER EYEWEAR

"... they look cool!"

One day back in the mid '80s master marketer Joseph Sugarman saw the future—and it was orange.

After leaving the U.S. Army, where he worked for both Army intelligence and the CIA, Sugarman became rich using print ads to hawk such "space age" doodads as calculators and digital watches. And in 1973 he and his Chicago-based company, IS&A Group, pioneered one of direct marketing's most important breakthroughs—offering 1–800 numbers for orders.

Always on the make for new items to peddle, Sugarman was visiting Los Angeles in 1986 when he inadvertently encountered a particularly spacey space-age creation. "I was driving with a manufacturer's rep to take a look at a new product, and he handed me a pair of sunglasses," he recalls. The specs that would change his life had orangish-looking lenses that screened out both blue and ultraviolet light. His driving companion said their manufacturer produced them using some sort of licensed NASA technology. But though the sales rep advised Sugarman to steer clear, he dropped a plug for the product into an airline promotional piece he was preparing. "I wrote the ad in

SINGING THE BLUS

Silverman's company, which initially spent about $1 million on magazine and newspaper promos, managed to sell a very respectable 100,000 BluBlockers in their first eight months on the market. Then came its television ad. Calling it a low-budget effort would be an insult to other low-budget efforts, yet in its first two months on the air the program moved an astonishing 100,000 pieces of product. So much for print.

all of two hours," he says. "They sold better than anything else in that particular insert."

Shortly thereafter Sugarman learned that the technology behind the pricey sunglasses wasn't on loan from NASA. Heck, it wasn't even protected by a patent. Which meant there was nothing to stop some enterprising individual (can you guess who?) from hooking up with an Asian manufacturer and producing a low-price version. In no time Sugarman created BluBlockers, named to emphasize their ability to block blu—oops, *blue*—light.

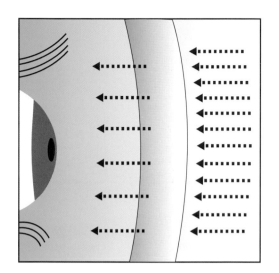

Blinded by the Light: The amber-colored lenses filter out blue and ultraviolet light, providing both superior eye protection and a distinctively '80s fashion statement.

THE BLUBLOCKErS BOOM

Back in the '80s if you wanted BluBlockers you could pick between a pair of *Top Gun*-ish aviator shades and a clip-on model for people with prescription glasses. "An infomercial will fail if the offer is too complicated," Sugarman says. "You can't offer several different styles of sunglasses to choose from. That will kill a commercial."

Sugarman stopped running infomercials in the early '90s, when rising prices for air time cut into profits. Not that his product went away. Today BluBlockers, freed from the TV-mandated need to keep things simple, are available on QVC and via retail in approximately one hundred different versions.

Buttoneer

"The problem with buttons is, they always fall off."

The Buttoneer sounds like the name of a third-rate superhero—the guy who gets the call when Superman is on a hot date with Lois Lane, Batman is washing his cowl, and Wonder Woman is speaking at a NOW rally.

But though the powers of this particular ASOTV product are limited, its longevity is truly superhuman. In a business where most products rise from nowhere, flit across our collective consciousness, and then disappear like last season's WB sitcoms, the Buttoneer—which burst on the scene decades ago—is still with us today.

Created by Massachusetts-based Dennison Manufacturing, a "global leader in pressure-sensitive technology," the Buttoneer is a staple, so to speak, of the company's fastener division—not to mention a fixture at your nearby Target or Walgreens. Users remove the protective covering from the two sharp pins located on the business end of the device, place one of the fasteners inside, rest the unit firmly in

THE PRODUCT

A device that reattaches buttons to garments via plastic paper clip–sized fasteners.

STATUS: On the market.

CLAIMED INNOVATION: Does away with needle and thread.

THE UPSIDE: Now any idiot can replace a button.

THE DOWNSIDE: Well, not quite any idiot. Novices will need several tries before they properly fasten a button. Still, it beats sewing.

NOT TO BE CONFUSED WITH

Musicians who play the Irish button accordion are also called buttoneers.

the palm, position the soon-to-be-fastened button, insert the pins into the buttonholes, and then pull back on the Buttoneer's pastel blue finger rests. Then, after that doesn't work, they insert another fastener and try again. Eventually it takes.

The marketing campaign wasn't an instant success, either. It took Ron Popeil to make the Buttoneer a household name. Approached by the manufacturer to make the product a hit, Popeil offered a simple but brilliant marketing strategy: Don't just identify the issue to be remedied, identify it repeatedly. His TV spot stated, "The problem with buttons is, they always fall off," then immediately echoed the same phrase. It went on to show how this agony (and in the commercial it really did seem like agony) could be forever ended with the purchase of one palm-sized, two-pronged plastic gizmo.

Looking like something Dr. McCoy would have used in a third-season *Star Trek* episode, the Buttoneer blossomed under Popeil's tutelage. Priced at $4.99, it sold some 200,000 units during its first Mother's Day on the market, then pushed three times as many over the holiday season.

Buttoneer Today

Rights for the invention eventually reverted back to Dennison Manufacturing boss Avery Dennison, who now sells it as The Original Buttoneer Fastening System. Each "system" contains the unit itself, plus a needle guard, 10 buttons, and 50 fasteners. If you rip off your shirt a lot (listen up, strippers and the Incredible Hulk), extra fasteners are sold separately.

While this device is the most high-profile member of the Buttoneer family, it's by no means the only member. Manufacturers make use of something called Buttoneer Tools—scissor-gripped gadgets used by the automobile industry to attach spacers to weather stripping in car doors. Because as we all know, the problem with weather stripping is, it always falls off.

Unauthorized Use

Attention groomsmen and prom kids: The buttoneer makes corsage application easy and fun. Removal is another matter.

FLOWBEE

"The advanced system that revolutionized the hair care industry."

One can only imagine the expressions on the faces of ASOTV buyers when they open the UPS box and get their first look at Flowbee. The first thing—practically the only thing—one sees after ripping open the not-meant-to-sell-in-stores packaging is rubber tubing. Miles, it seems, of rubber tubing. Like darkened intestine it coils around itself, concealing the bright yellow and clear plastic pieces that fill out the package. Have the Flowbee people accidentally sent car parts?

Nope, they've sent you a one-of-a-kind device that makes having your hair cut at home even more humiliating than it already is.

The Flowbee system was invented by carpenter Rick Hunt, who got the idea when he noticed how efficiently an industrial vacuum sucked sawdust from his hair (must have been a slow day at the lumber mill). By connecting an electric razor to an ordinary household vacuum cleaner, Hunt pioneered the goofiest ASOTV creation since the Chia Pet.

One thing that sets Flowbee apart from other products is that it seems to violate the "Wouldn't it be great if . . ." principle. New products (usually) must fill some unlooked-for niche: Wouldn't it be great if I could put a button on without sewing? Wouldn't it be great if I could

THE PRODUCT

A haircutting system that hooks up to a home vacuum cleaner.

STATUS: On the market.

CLAIMED INNOVATION: No-mess haircuts.

THE UPSIDE: Mess-free and, if used properly, allows for regular same-length trims.

THE DOWNSIDE: You must know something about haircutting, lest your victims look like they lost a fight with a ceiling fan.

SPIN-OFFS

The Flowbee Pet Groomer brings the money-saving magic of home hair care to the animal kingdom. But don't try it on a collie, because Flowbee doesn't work on hair longer than six inches. And given many pets' violent hatred of vacuum cleaners, you might want to put on oven mitts and a catcher's mask before starting.

40

make the perfect omelet in the microwave? Wouldn't it be great if my abs looked like the guys' on the cover of *Men's Health*?

The Flowbee doesn't do this. Instead it makes three very large, very dicey assumptions about the American consumer. First, that a significant number of people cut their own hair or the hair of family members. Second, that those people would just love to use something besides standard scissors and clippers. And third (this is the big one), that the biggest perceived obstacle to home haircutting isn't the skill of the cutter, but the mess caused by fallen hair.

Incredibly, enough people bought into Assumption No. 3 to make the Flowbee a winner. The product has racked up more than $25 million in sales and as of 2002 was still moving about 9,000 units a year. That's a lot of activity for something that, at press time, sold for a fairly steep $69.95 plus postage and handling.

Test case

"Congratulations," reads the opening line of the Flowbee User's Guide. "You have just purchased a most revolutionary haircutting device. . . . Count on a perfect, fast, precise haircut every time with virtually no cleanup."

Well . . . okay. We get the "no cleanup" part. That's why the clipping device is attached to a vacuum cleaner. If it wasn't neat, it would be grounds for calling the Better Business Bureau. But how can they guarantee a "perfect" or "precise" haircut? Don't people go to beauty school for years (or at least months) just to do a competent job at The Hair Cuttery?

We assume children are the main targets of Flowbee users because they're the only segment of the population that can be legally forced to sit still for it. And yet the Flowbee booklet, Web site, and infomercial persist in showing people cutting their own hair. Take that with a grain of salt. Remember, infomercials also show people who are pee-their-pants excited over food dehydrators.

The Rules

According to the instructional booklet, all you have to do to become the next Vidal Sassoon is attach Flowbee to a vacuum cleaner, familiarize yourself with the plastic spacers that snap onto the cutting head, and follow such helpful hints as:

* **Start with the top of the head.**

    Turn the Flowbee on and cut until you have achieved the desired length.
* **Cut the entire head a little at a time to yield the most gradual, even look.**
* **You may wish to use a little scissor trimming around the edges after cutting with the Flowbee system.**

They could also add, "You may wish to consider home schooling for your child, because his oddball Flowbee haircut will probably draw the attention of playground bullies and, if it's particularly heinous, child welfare authorities."

GLH FORMULA #9

"Hair in a can."

Like that other brilliant import, Nad's hair removal gel (see page 48), GLH Formula #9 was created in Australia. You've got to admire the quirkiness of those Down Under inventors. Instead of pioneering, say, new energy sources, they seem consumed by body hair issues—how to remove it from inappropriate places and, in the case of GLH, how to spray it on others.

To be fair, GLH is technically not spray paint. According to the ad, "It's an amazing powder that clings to the tiniest hairs on your head." Kind of like useful lice. It's suitable for both men and women—albeit to roughly the same degree that fishing shows are suitable for both men and women. Distributor Ron Popeil claims the product works on bald spots big or small; fine or thinning hair; gray hair that pops up between colorings; the plugs and patches of hair transplant patients; and for those using Minoxidil or other hair replacement drugs.

Applying GLH isn't all that different from spray painting your gang sign on a bridge abutment. First shake the can vigorously, hold it no more than three or four inches away from the bald spot, and fire away. Keep a hand mirror and a wall mirror handy, lest you accidentally coat your ears. Once you've applied enough

THE PRODUCT

An aerosol spray that covers bald spots.

STATUS: On the market.

CLAIMED INNOVATION: Cheaper than a hair weave.

THE UPSIDE: Works as advertised, but only if you have very low expectations.

THE DOWNSIDE: Get found out and you might as well have written LOSER on your forehead.

coverage (how this is determined is up to you), it's time to preserve your Lichtenstein-like effort by lacquering on a coat of Finishing Shield.

Now you're a teenager again—albeit a teenager who can't touch his new "do" for five minutes or take a shower without having it swirl down the drain in a black stream like Janet Leigh's blood in *Psycho*. There are other caveats as well. If your snappy new look earns you an overnighter, keep in mind that the powder could make its way, mascara-like, from your head to the pillow. In theory it could, from there, attach to your partner's face. Again, in theory, you could go to bed with a Heather Locklear look-alike and wake up with a chimney sweep.

Of course this isn't very likely—especially the part about someone wearing GLH getting in bed with a beautiful woman. Rest assured, however, that any stains caused by GLH are, like the effect it produces, fleeting. If your dome accidentally comes in contact with, say, leather furniture, the blemish it leaves can be removed by whatever product one normally uses to clean that surface.

REFILLS

A can of GLH is good for about 30 applications. Then you have to seal it in a discreet bag before depositing it in the trash, lest the garbage man laugh at you. Regular losers—oops, *users*—can join the GLH Club and buy in bulk.

POP QUESTION

WHAT DOES THE #9 IN GLH FORMULA #9 STAND FOR? IS IT THE NUMBER OF PEOPLE WHO'VE ACTUALLY FOOLED SOMEONE WITH THIS PRODUCT?

It's just another example of Popeil's promotional prowess. Back at the dawn of his sales career when he worked at a Chicago Woolworth's store, he heard about a man who enjoyed huge success with a beauty product called Charles Antel Formula #9. If the number was good enough for that guy, it was good enough for Popeil, who without further ceremony tacked it onto his product.

THE GLH QUOTE BOOK

"You know who would be a great candidate for this? Al Gore."
—Ron Popeil, quoted in *The New Yorker*

Hairagami

"Experience the art of folding hair."

The world of weird hairstyles owes a huge debt to Princess Leia. What female, when she first saw *Star Wars*, didn't gaze longingly at Carrie Fisher's hair and wish that she too could walk around with cinnamon rolls strapped to her head?

Today, achieving such otherworldly coifs has never been easier, thanks to the latest advance in Odd Hair Technology, Hairagami. Sporting a logo that looks like the snakes from the American Medical Association logo doing the nasty with the Nabisco symbol, the system promises to transform your hair just as radically as the Japanese art of origami transforms paper. Although you can't use it to make a crane out of your tresses, you can come darn close. Each cleverly designed kit contains four Hairagamis (which look like fuzzy tongue depressors), a Snap-Action Scrunchie (didn't Diana Rigg pack one of those on *The Avengers*?), a 32-page Glamour Guide, and an instructional video (alas, you don't get the video in the store-bought version).

THE PRODUCT

Twisty things that make it easy (or rather, easier) to achieve extreme hairstyling effects.

STATUS: On the market.

CLAIMED INNOVATION: Spring-action technology keeps elaborate dos in place.

THE UPSIDE: They do indeed create peculiar hairstyles—provided the subject has long, straight hair.

THE DOWNSIDE: They do indeed create peculiar hairstyles.

The Hairagamis serve as the stiff framework for massive updo looks, the scrunchie as the foundation for ponytailed styles. But don't think you'll be an expert all at once. The Glamour Guide, anticipating your frustration, offers a quote from an anonymous user that seems targeted to allay new-buyer angst. "Although it was awkward at first," the quote reads, "after I learned how to control the spring, Hairagami allowed me to style my hair in ways that I have never seen before."

No argument there. As one would expect, many of the somewhat tortured-looking effects achieved by Hairagami seem to fall outside the boundaries of mainstream taste and style. Fortunately for the manufacturer, a great many American consumers fall outside those boundaries as well. How else to explain the fact that the product, launched in 2000, grew

rapidly from an "order now" fixture to a "prominently displayed at Target" best-seller? It's quite an achievement for a system that, in its own promotional materials, shows adults affecting high-rise hairstyles rarely seen outside of under-21 clubs or Starfleet Academy class photos. Hairagami's packaging proudly states that the system is for ages 8 to 108, but it's hard to imagine one of Willard Scott's birthday centenarians folding, wrapping, and snapping her way to such never-in-style styles as the Chinese Fan or the Forget Me Knot.

> "The 'Flip' technology is a multi-sensory technology. You can see it. You can feel it. You can hear it."
> —Hairagami Web site

Hairagami Trivia

For reasons we'll never understand, the Snap-Action Scrunchie was originally called "Hairagami Pony."

The Sequel

"Want to know the secret art of getting that Hollywood part?" the folks who brought you Hairagami ask. Ignoring the obvious follow-up question (What the hell is a "Hollywood part?"), Part Pizazz offers the answer. This kit features all the "tools" (including one that looks like chopsticks designed by someone on acid) needed to draw "illusion parts," "broken parts," and "zigzags" across your scalp, revealing areas of your head that haven't seen the light of day since Mom raked them with a lice comb. According to the package the Part Pizazz is for ages 5 to 105, which lets your first grader in on the fun but denies it to your 106-year-old aunt.

LifeCall Alert System

"Help! I've fallen and I can't get up!"

Remember Edith Fore?

Probably not. But while few can recall her name, almost everyone recognizes her claim to fame. The single sentence she uttered during a commercial for a home security device called the LifeCall Alert System has become an indelible part of television advertising history, right alongside "Where's the beef?"

Fore's famous words were, "Help! I've fallen and I can't get up!" The line quickly insinuated its way into speeches, political cartoons, and late-night monologues. It formed the punchline of numberless dirty jokes and was even honored by *TV Guide* as the seventh catchiest ad since the creation of the cathode-ray tube.

Incredibly, the ad was no mere acting job. It was, instead, a testimonial. Fore, who got $500 for her efforts, was actually saved by the LifeCall Alert

THE PRODUCT

An emergency contact device connecting clients to a central command post.

STATUS: Off the market.

CLAIMED INNOVATION: An electronic lifeline for seniors and the infirm.

THE UPSIDE: Instant help in emergencies.

THE DOWNSIDE: Well, not quite instant. Someone had to call to determine the nature of the problem, then dispatch police or an ambulance, yada, yada, yada . . .

UNAUTHORIZED USE

Curing one's loneliness by talking to a nice stranger.

System when she fell and hit her head while home alone. Bleeding, she made the famous plea. "They saved her life that day," her daughter, Pat Logan, told a New Jersey newspaper. In fact, after so many people made light of her plight, LifeCall felt obliged to issue a follow-up commercial featuring Fore (now safely vertical) explaining that she wasn't kidding—she really had fallen.

Soon Fore—who, though she had trouble getting up, seemed to have no trouble getting around—hit the media circuit. And so the former school nurse became a news sensation. She chalked up appearances on 70 radio programs and several TV shows and scored write-ups in magazines such as *People*, which profiled her in 1990.

While the ad drew lots of attention, it failed to attract customers. Fore's famous words are still fondly recalled by millions of couch potatoes, but few can remember the product her pleading was meant to endorse. Despite a killer ad, LifeCall went bankrupt and fell into the hands of Trenton, New Jersey–based Response USA. As for Edith Fore, she died in 1997 at Our Lady of Lourdes Medical Center in Camden, New Jersey, at the age of 81.

THE LOST TRANSCRIPTS

After Edith Fore passed away, Comedy Central's *The Daily Show* offered this invented sound bite of her "actual" unedited phone call.

"I've fallen! I'm bleeding!"

"And . . . what can't you do?"

"I . . . can't get to the phone?"

"Nooo . . ."

"Help, I'm dying!"

"Just say the words. Now what have you done?"

"I've fallen!"

"And?"

"I'm bleeding?"

"No! Just say the words! Say the words, dammit! Say it!"

"I've fallen and I can't get up!"

"Bingo! There's a good girl. Okay, the camera crew will be there in 15 minutes."

SPIN-OFFS

Edith Fore performed overdubbed vocals on the "Can't Watch This" cut on the Weird Al Yankovich album *Off the Deep End*. Also, country singer Charlie Floyd recorded a song titled "I've Fallen in Love (And I Can't Get Up)." And Pastor T. D. Jakes penned an inspirational tome called *Help Me: I've Fallen & I Can't Get Up*.

NAD'S

"The Aussies have gone mad for Nad's."

"What's in a name?" asks Shakespeare's Juliet, implying that the titles we give to people and objects don't sum up their true nature. That simple sentiment is horrifically illustrated by Nad's, a hair-removal compound that's easily the worst-named product in the infomercial universe.

While the mere mention of the word makes the casual observer think of male naughty bits, we can assure you that Nad's has nothing to do with that. Or rather, those. Nad's is a sticky, gross-smelling, spinach-colored goo that looks like the stuff they drop on kids' heads during game shows on Nickelodeon. Users smear a thin layer on a hairy portion of the body, cover the mess with a cloth strip, and then rip it away. Consumers can even reuse the very same strip within 20 seconds—provided they can wipe the tears from their eyes and squelch their screaming in the allotted time. That's because unlike other hair removal products, Nad's doesn't "melt" hair or cause it to fall out on its own. It tears it out by the roots.

Like the hair-adding GLH Formula #9 (see page 42), Nad's is a product of Australia where, surprisingly

THE PRODUCT

An all-natural, no-heat hair removal gel.

STATUS: On the market.

CLAIMED INNOVATION: No hair for four to six weeks.

THE UPSIDE: It really does take off hair.

THE DOWNSIDE: So does a blowtorch—and with slightly less pain.

APPLY, SCREAM, REPEAT

The manufacturers recommend reapplying the slime every three to six weeks.

enough, it was not developed as a prisoner interrogation aid. In fact, its creation was something of a humanitarian effort. A Sydney woman named Sue Ismiel concocted it in order to tame the thick hair sprouting from the arms and legs of her 6-year-old daughter, Natalie.

"Although she said she was never teased at school, I knew she had low self-esteem," says Ismiel in official Nad's materials. "She wanted to be a model, but I knew how self-conscious she was. She insisted on wearing long-sleeved clothing." Sensitive mom Ismiel looked around for a product to make poor Natalie look less Cousin It-ish. Dissatisfied with store-bought remedies, she knocked together the first batch of Nad's in her kitchen, combining ingredients that make it sound like a juice bar's version of a Hairy Buffalo—a mix of honey, molasses, lemon juice, fructose, water, alcohol, and food dye. Of course, test subject No. 1 was poor little hirsute Natalie.

"That didn't hurt at all, Mummy," the girl reportedly said after her first treatment.

Hmmm. We sense a *Mommie Dearest*–style tell-all book in her future.

NO, IT'S NOT A MISUNDERSTANDING

More than one casual viewer has wondered if, just perhaps, "nads" means something different in Australia than it does here. No such luck. This is the definition offered in the *American-Australian Slang Dictionary*: nads n. (Always plural; contraction of gonads). Testicles (s.a. ball).

WHAT DOES THE NAME REALLY MEAN?

Nad's is named after creator Sue Ismiel's other daughter, Nadine. So why didn't Mom name it after Natalie, the subject of her experiments? If she had, people around the world would be smearing Nat's on themselves.

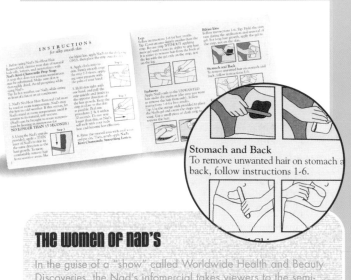

Stomach and Back
To remove unwanted hair on stomach a
back, follow instructions 1-6.

THE WOMEN OF NAD'S

In the guise of a "show" called Worldwide Health and Beauty Discoveries, the Nad's infomercial takes viewers to the semi-wilds of Australia, where hostess Denise Krueger conducts what amounts to an ex-werewolf encounter group with a batch of female Nad's fans. The women all seem to share a hemophiliac's dread of using razors, along with a Howard Hughes–like terror of being seen in public. "I could go out of the house immediately after using Nad's," says one shut-in, "which is great." Based on their comments, it's clear they're battling problems far beyond monobrows and chin fuzz.

Interspersed among the testimonials are shot after shot of Nad's-encrusted cloths tearing hair off arms, legs, and, in one very memorable scene, a back that could easily belong to a male lowland gorilla. Subjects for these demos seem to have been selected for their pain tolerance. They never flinch, even as beaver-pelt-size swaths of hair are ripped from their persons.

TURBIE TWIST

"Looks chic!"

Comedians since time immemorial have pointed out that manufacturers still deem it necessary to print the instructions, "Lather. Rinse. Repeat," on shampoo bottles. The same mentality seems to have infected the makers of the Turbie Twist, which takes the relatively simple task of swathing one's still-wet hair in a towel and makes it, well, relatively simpler. Of course, generations of people with long, wet hair have coped with this "problem" in the same basic way—take a towel, wrap it around your head, tuck it into some sort of genie-type covering and then go about your business. Now, however, the geniuses at Smart Inventions, Inc. have developed a new wet hair management technique that's light years beyond the standard terry cloth towel.

Their replacement?

A standard terry cloth towel.

Well, sort of. Thanks to a specially designed elastic loop, the Turbie Twist claims to be the head towel of the twenty-first century. You can't roll this one up and smack your locker room buddies on the tush with it, but you can stop worrying about whether the makeshift knot you use to bind a traditional towel to your head will come undone as you go about your

THE PRODUCT

A towel with an elastic loop.

STATUS: On the market.

CLAIMED INNOVATION: Stays on your head.

THE UPSIDE: Like we just said, it stays on your head.

THE DOWNSIDE: So do most towels—and they don't get lost in the laundry pile as easily as Turbie Twist.

UNAUTHORIZED USE

Key element in do-it-yourself Erykah Badu Halloween costume.

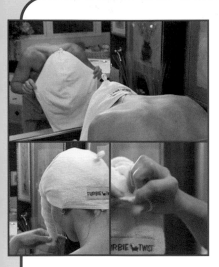

business. With the Turbie Twist you can do housework, rearrange your sock drawer, or give come-hither looks to the UPS guy (a situation that's actually recreated in the product's infomercial) without worrying about embarrassing towel flaccidity. All you have to do is place it on your head so that the length of the towel and your hair both dangle in front of your face. Just twist the two together and place the roll on top of your head, pulling the tip through the loop.

There. Now you look like the woman on the front of the Turbie Twist box. And both of you look like Mama Smurf.

A FEW WORDS ABOUT OVERSTATEMENT

The words "Looks chic" are emblazoned on the Turbie Twist packaging. One must look to the pages of George Orwell's *1984* to find similarly brazen defilements of the English language. Turbie Twist may dry hair. It may stay securely on your head. But until we see a model parading down a Paris runway while wearing one, we refuse to call it "chic."

MS. TURBIE

Let us now praise the real star of the Turbie Twist infomercial, Darla Haun. Yes, there are beautiful women out there in ASOTV Land, but those who are certifiably hot usually push a product—breast enhancement pills, exercise gizmos—that invites ogling. But Haun, referred to on her own Web site as "The New Millennium Woman," manages to make unattractive head coverings somehow provocative. Maybe it's her acting range. Of course she's no Meryl Streep, but she boasts a resume (featured in the computer game *Timelapse*, in the Mel Brooks movie *Dracula: Dead and Loving It*, and in 29 episodes of something called *The Sci-Fi Trader*) that makes her sound like a Juilliard graduate compared to other TV shills. If *Response* magazine, the Bible of the electronic retailing biz, ever publishes a swimsuit issue, Haun should be on the cover.

part 3
FABULOUS fitness

Name just about any physical shortcoming and
you can bet there's an ASOTV product or person
ready to roll, sweat, flex, or shock it out of existence.
To unlock your body's potential we proudly offer the
infomercial stylings of Soloflex, Richard Simmons,
NordicTrack, Dr. Ho, and many, many more.

ABTRONIC

"The future of fitness."

One need only look at the cover of *Men's Health* magazine—any cover—to understand the importance of rock-hard abs in today's society. But creating that six-pack midsection on your own isn't easy, and advertisers know it. Why else would half the info-mercials in existence deal with this fitness dilemma?

The airwaves are filled with pitches for ab devices, which leads to the obvious question: Which one works best? We don't have a clue. But we do know the one that demands the least effort—so little, in fact, that puffy, lardy TV viewers can actually use it while parked on the couch watching TV. That humble little device is a technological wonder called the Abtronic.

Far from looking like a piece of exercise equipment, the Abtronic is simply a strap-on electrical patch that resembles a petite version of the massive belts worn by weight lifters. The device uses contact pads (smeared with a slimy gel that's necessary to establish conductivity) to electrically stimulate the abs, causing them to flex spasmodically. This process, according to the Abtronic folks, gives one a "workout" equivalent to what you'd receive if you got down on the floor and used those "other" ab machines.

THE PRODUCT

A strap-on belt that electrically stimulates muscles.

STATUS: On the market.

CLAIMED INNOVATION: Get a six-pack without exercise.

THE UPSIDE: Compact. Lightweight.

THE DOWNSIDE: They don't work—or at least that's what the government says. In early 2002 the Federal Trade Commision filed false advertising complaints against Abtronic and two other manufactureres of electronic "exercise" belts.

The Abtronic is small enough to wear under your clothes so that, in theory, while the rest of your associates are crunching numbers, you can crunch off last night's extra bag of Doritos. Friends may wonder why your shirt is vibrating, but trust us on this one, they won't ask.

Unlike most exercise contraptions that gracefully retire to the garage when their noble work is done, the Abtronic has a natural life span, estimated by the manufacturers to be about 400 uses. How do you know it's ready for the great gym in the sky? "If you get a tingling sensation but which is coming more from the center rather than from the sides of the Neoprene Center piece," the instructions awkwardly state, "this is an indication that your Neoprene Center piece is worn out."

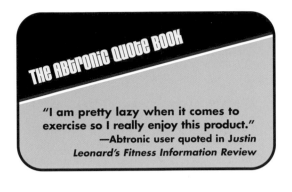

THE ABTRONIC QUOTE BOOK

"I am pretty lazy when it comes to exercise so I really enjoy this product."
—Abtronic user quoted in *Justin Leonard's Fitness Information Review*

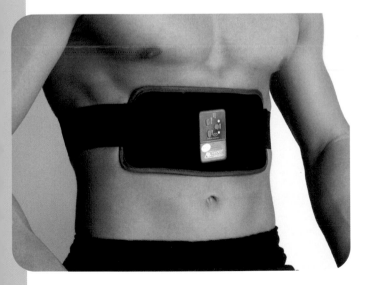

IT'S AN AB WORLD AFTER ALL

Tired of the Abtronic? Then perhaps its time to move on to another belly cruncher. To unlock your body's potential, we proudly offer . . . the AbEnergizer, the Abdoer, the Rio Ab Belt, the Ab Lifter Plus, the Ab Away Pro, the Ab Dolly, the Ab Flex, the Ab Force, Ab Rocker, Ab Roller, Ab Sculptor, Ab Slide, Ab Twister, Abaratus, and Fast Abs. When, oh when, will some tinkerer create a kids' exercise device called the Lil' Ab-ner?

BODY BY JAKE

"Don't quit."

If Goldilocks needed a fitness guru she'd probably pick Jake "Body by Jake" Steinfeld. While Richard Simmons is a bit too wired, and ponytailed Tony Little is *way* too scary, Steinfeld's semi-laid-back persona seems just right. Compared to most of TV's shouting, preening, can't-stand-still-for-a-minute "fitness entrepreneurs," the man who brought us the Ab Rocker and the Bun & Thigh Rocker seems—dare we say it—almost mellow.

Maybe he's so reticent because of the stuttering problem he battled while growing up on Long Island. He started improving his self-esteem (along with his delts and glutes) when his father gave him a weight set at age 13. Steinfeld pumped up and in 1977 moved to California to pursue a common childhood fantasy: becoming Mr. America. But that dream quickly died when he learned he couldn't do it without a little help from Mr. Steroids. Disillusioned, he sought work on the fringes of the entertainment industry, serving as Lou Ferrigno's stunt double on *The Incredible Hulk*. And then fate (in the form of a model who hired him to help her tone up for a commercial) intervened. Steinfeld whipped the woman into shape under the appreciative eyes of her boyfriend, who turned out to be director Francis Ford Coppola. Before you could say "networking" he was performing similar fitness

THE PRODUCT

The Bun & Thigh Rocker, which uses rubber resistance bands like Soloflex (see page 68) to build one's lower extremities.

STATUS: On the market.

CLAIMED INNOVATION: Efficient development of the legs and "buttisimo."

THE UPSIDE: It works as long as you use it.

THE DOWNSIDE: No matter how toned you become, you'll still look like a dork while riding the thing.

SPIN-OFFS

A couple of years ago Steinfeld, a former college lacrosse player at Cortland State University, founded a new athletic league called Major League Lacrosse. At press time, the six-team operation played in such "hotbeds" of the sport as Islip, New York; Bridgeport, Connecticut; and Montclair, New Jersey.

services (at a greatly increased fee) for the likes of Steven Spielberg, Harrison Ford, and Bette Midler.

In 1980 Steinfeld established Body by Jake Enterprises. Today he sells everything from vitamins to workout tapes to the aforementioned Bun & Thigh Rocker, for which the infomercial features a cast big enough to rival that of a DeMille movie.

But even though Steinfeld can't seem to make it through a single on-air sentence without either saying "don't quit" or mentioning "the ol' buttisimo" (his personal catchphrase for the derriere), he's by far the least grating of TV's Spandex-swathed sultans of sweat.

THE BODY BY JAKE QUOTE BOOK

"Hey guys, imagine having the kind of buttisimo that turns the girls' heads."
—Steinfeld during the Bun & Thigh Rocker infomercial

Interesting, Impossible-to-Verify Claim

Steinfeld states that he invented the phrase "personal trainer."

POP QUESTION

DIDN'T I SEE JAKE IN A MOVIE?

This Jake of all trades landed roles in the Eddie Murphy vehicle *Coming to America*; *The Money Pit* with Tom Hanks; and *Cheech & Chong's Next Movie*. He also played the villain in a low-budget slasher pic called *Home Sweet Home* and starred in a short-lived TV sitcom *Big Brother Jake*.

Dr-Ho's muscle massage system

"You don't need tension, you need Dr. Ho now."

"Dr. Ho" sounds like either a pornographic sendup of the James Bond movie *Dr. No* or the name of a supporting character in a '70s blaxploitation flick. But it's really the moniker of Michael Ho, doctor of chiropractic and acupuncture and director of the Toronto Pain and Headache Clinic. His slightly twisted claim to fame? Using bikini babes to advance the concept of better living through shock therapy.

Ho helped invent, and lent his name to, a device that "massages" muscles via electric stimulation. Chiropractors are big on this technique, which is called "electronic impulse therapy." But Ho, who was reportedly dissatisfied with existing technology and its short-lived benefits, developed (with the help of engineers) a system that varies the speed and frequency of the stimulation, allegedly making it more effective. All you have to do is apply gel-filled pads to the afflicted area, run the electrodes back to the main unit, and cut loose with the juice.

THE PRODUCT

An electrical unit that delivers low-voltage charges to isolated portions of the body, causing the muscles located there to repeatedly contract and relax.

STATUS: On the market.

CLAIMED INNOVATION: Get a relaxing electrical massage at home.

THE UPSIDE: Only $99.99 for the starter kit.

THE DOWNSIDE: Is there such a thing as a "relaxing electrical massage?"

SPIN-OFFS

You can also purchase, for the low, low price of $79.99, an orthopedic sleep aid called the Ho Fun Pillow. Really.

Here's where the bikini babes come in. Ho's first infomercial showed the good doctor lounging with a bevy of hot females as he enthusiastically explained what his machine did. He even applied the gel packs to parts of his own body, which promptly started jumping around like hooked trout.

Interestingly, all that physical commotion is caused by the two measly AA batteries powering the system. That means customers can't be seriously injured by the device, unless they somehow manage to strangle themselves with the electrical leads. In case you're worried, just check out Dr. Ho's Web page, which is infused with the same enthusiastic but slightly incoherent tone of the man himself. It states, among many other things, that the system gives "Dramatic relieve for muscle tension," but warns that you shouldn't "temper with it in any way" and to "consult medical attention" if problems arise.

POWER TO THE PEOPLE

The jury is out—*waaay* out—on the usefulness of electrical muscle stimulation for most problems. However, this doesn't stop Ho's Web page from posting customer testimonials stating that the machine has alleviated such ailments as migraines, neck pain, foot pain, tendonitis, sciatica, bursitis, menstrual cramps, whiplash, carpal tunnel syndrome, stress-related insomnia, and many, many more. Apparently, clients believe very strongly in the device—so strongly that Ho feels it necessary to warn them not to try it on open wounds.

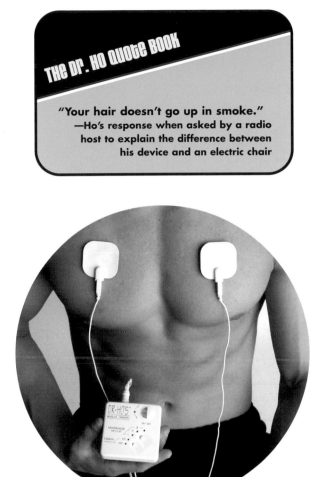

THE DR. HO QUOTE BOOK

"Your hair doesn't go up in smoke."
—Ho's response when asked by a radio host to explain the difference between his device and an electric chair

SO WHAT'S IT FEEL LIKE?

Sort of a tickling sensation, like a low-voltage electrical shock—which is, of course, exactly what it is.

TONY LITTLE'S GAZELLE FREESTYLE

"America's Personal Trainer.™"

The real star of the widely viewed Gazelle Freestyle infomercial isn't the device—a trapeze-like affair with ski pole handles that let the user walk or run without actually touching the ground. It's the product's promoter, leather-lunged fitness impresario Tony Little. You may not know the name, but you'd recognize his massive blond ponytail, in-your-face "motivational techniques," and action-figure physique anywhere.

America's Personal Trainer™ got his start as a professional bodybuilder. But then, according to his bio, he was sidelined in 1985 by a car accident. Despondent, he porked out, got depressed and, for some reason, spent a great deal of time watching celebrity workout videos. Unimpressed with what he found, he got his act together, made his own tape, and, in 1987, got airtime on the Home Shopping Network. He sold all 500 copies in just a few minutes, beginning a decade-long relationship with HSN. Through the channel he's hawked exercise videos, clothing, equipment, vitamins, and even his own magazine.

But Little really comes into his own during his infomercials—particularly the one for the Gazelle. From the moment he's introduced by his cohost, spokesbabe

THE PRODUCT

A low-impact exercise machine with foot pads suspended about a foot off the ground.

STATUS: On the market.

CLAIMED INNOVATION: Provides an extremely low-impact aerobic workout.

THE UPSIDE: It works.

THE DOWNSIDE: So does regular walking.

Darla Haun (see page 51), it's clear that he should have spent a few minutes on one of his machines, burning off excess energy, before the cameras rolled. While Haun, decked out in skintight "sweats," smiles, nods, and fawns, Little dashes from one end of the set to the other, knocking papers off a display table and climbing over obstacles like an inmate at the Yerkes Primate Institute. More than once his "high-energy" personality drifts into the annoying zone—like when he scrambles onto a demonstration dais, gets in the face of a Gazelle-riding male model, and yells, "Hi Tom!" in the sort of volume usually reserved for hailing New York City cabs.

There must be a market for this, or else Little, as his infomercial states, wouldn't have won 10 platinum and eight gold video awards—whatever those are. And he wouldn't have sold millions of dollars worth of exercise gear. And he wouldn't be so sure of his status as America's Personal Trainer™ that he felt the need to trademark the phrase.

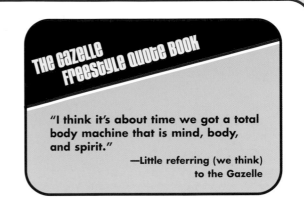

The Gazelle Freestyle Quote Book

"I think it's about time we got a total body machine that is mind, body, and spirit."

—Little referring (we think) to the Gazelle

Beauty and the Ponytailed Beast

Little's infomercial cohost is the lovely and semi-talented Darla Haun, the same ASOTV diva who also graces the Turbie Twist campaign (see page 51). Smiling like a Miss America contestant throughout the program, she steals the show when she strips down to her sports bra and goes hell-for-leather on the Gazelle.

The Tony Little Collection

Before the Gazelle there was Tony Little's ABS Only Machine (one of the dozens of rocker-type crunch devices on the market a few years back). He's also got a slew of workout videos, most with names so no-nonsense and hyperdescriptive they could have been issued by the Marines. Take, for example, *Target Training No Impact Hips, Buttocks, and Thighs—Volume II* and *Total Body Weight Loss Video*. Many of the tape boxes feature Little and a luscious female model, with America's Personal Trainer™ either pointing to or actually touching the part of the model's body the tape is designed to help.

nOrDicTrack

"Ski your way to a beautiful body."

Back at the dawn of the infomercial age, two products vied for different portions of the home fitness biz. While Soloflex (see page 68) cornered the market for muscle-building machines, Minneapolis-based NordicTrack took the cardio workout world by storm.

The two accomplished this by offering what was then a novelty—full-size home exercise systems that broke down into compact, easy-to-store shapes when not in use. As the world already knows, NordicTrack's other brainstorm was to simulate cross-country skiing using a patented flywheel system that could produce varying levels of resistance. Users donned their tights and leg warmers, seized the handgrips that stood in for ski poles, locked their feet into the tracks, and went to town, striding through a low-impact workout.

During the late '80s and early '90s this simple device (and the tasteful infomercials that accompanied it) transformed the company from a 95-pound weakling into a fitness heavyweight racking up $400 million in annual sales. But then came the attack of the clones. By the mid-'90s the home exercise market was overrun with Flexes and Tracks and Gliders, leaving the original ski machine little breathing room. The once-proud firm became a unit of Massachusetts-based CML Group, dismissed hundreds of employees, closed

THE PRODUCT

A home exercise machine that simulates cross-country skiing.

STATUS: On the market (see sidebar on next page).

CLAIMED INNOVATION: Offered a novel (at the time) aerobic workout.

THE UPSIDE: Was low-impact when low-impact wasn't cool.

THE DOWNSIDE: The alternating arms-and-legs striding motion required a good deal of coordination.

a Minnesota manufacturing plant, and shut down catalog sales—all to no avail. In 1998 NordicTrack filed for bankruptcy, followed shortly thereafter by CML itself.

THE END OF NORDICTRACK . . . NOT

When NordicTrack's parent company pulled the plug, it sold its inventory and trademarks to Utah-based Icon Health & Fitness, a firm that touts itself as the world's largest manufacturer and marketer of home fitness equipment. Under its guidance the NordicTrack brand has, if not exactly thrived, at least stabilized. One can even buy the original NordicTrack machine, now called the Classic Pro Skier.

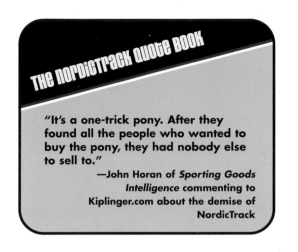

THE NORDICTRACK QUOTE BOOK

"It's a one-trick pony. After they found all the people who wanted to buy the pony, they had nobody else to sell to."

—John Horan of *Sporting Goods Intelligence* commenting to Kiplinger.com about the demise of NordicTrack

POP QUESTION

IS IT A GOOD WORKOUT?

Sure . . . though not quite as good as NordicTrack once claimed. In 1996 the company settled an FCC lawsuit stating that it made "false and unsubstantiated weight loss and weight maintenance claims in advertising its cross-country ski exercise machine."

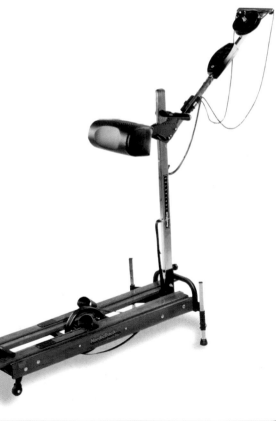

NOT A QUIET WORKOUT

One dig against the original system was that it made more noise than a threshing machine. Some models included a book rest, perhaps because the noise made watching TV next to impossible.

Susan Powter

"Stop the insanity!"

Remember the documentary *Scared Straight*, in which frightened teens were locked inside a men's prison with scary-looking inmates so they could see what hard time was really like? Dieters got a similarly masochistic experience by watching the over-the-top antics of early '90s exercise guru Susan Powter. Sporting short-cropped blond hair that made her look like a Barbie doll run over by a lawn mower, Powter burst upon the scene screaming "Stop the insanity!" and promoting a program of sensible exercise and eating.

Given her unsettling intensity and bizarre looks, the casual channel surfer would be forgiven for thinking he'd tuned into an exorcism instead of an exercise session. He wouldn't have been far from wrong, considering the personal demons Powter battled. Like other great infomercial workout celebs (see Richard Simmons, page 66, and Tony Little, page 60), she was a former plus-sizer on a mission. "I got fat because I ate tons of high-fat food, stopped moving, and ignored my body," she declared before preaching a gospel that showed devotees how to ixnay the atfay.

Unlike typical exercise tapes that feature more hot bodies than a *Girls Gone Wild* video (see page 96), Powter peopled her sessions with women from across

THE PRODUCT

Exercise videotapes.

STATUS: On the market.

CLAIMED INNOVATION: No-nonsense advice that stands up to the multimillion-dollar diet industry.

THE UPSIDE: Powter raises some meaningful questions about the proper way to diet and exercise.

THE DOWNSIDE: If you can lose weight and look great and still be this uptight and angry, why bother?

the girth spectrum—including some so big they looked like they should be floating over football stadiums. The message was that workouts weren't just for the already trim. The subtext: My God, you don't ever want to look like *that*.

America proved receptive to the power of Powter, who spent her 15 minutes of fame working her mouth as vigorously as her body. She attacked the diet industry. She attacked the gym industry. She mocked the quest for model-like physiques. She even blasted the scheduled feeding of babies. But like most people who talk too loud, she quickly lost her audience. The world moved on, leaving Powter to fight her own personal, familial, and legal struggles—and also, finally, to grow her hair out.

POP-UP POWTER

Susan Powter guest starred on *The Fresh Prince of Bel-Air* as herself, on *Space Ghost Coast to Coast* as herself, and on the short-lived Delta Burke sitcom *Women of the House* as Janet Block. She briefly hosted her own television motivational show in 1974.

THE SUSAN POWTER QUOTE BOOK

"Going from the topless dancer to the owner of a corporation is a big transition."
—Powter in her book *Stop the Insanity!*

LIVE THE INSANITY!

Raised in a Dominican convent in Sydney, Australia, Powter relocated to Garland, Texas. There she married, had two kids, found out her husband was unfaithful, separated, dove head-first into a bottomless bag of pork rinds, divorced, and then puffed up to more than 260 pounds. Lithium and Bible study groups failed to lift her mood, so she left her kids with her ex-husband and took off for California.

Once there, Powter slimmed down, hacked her hair, and opened her own exercise studio. Infomercial fame followed. She rented a nearby apartment for her ex and the kids, remarried, this time to a guitar player, and adopted another child. Marriage No. 2 lasted six years, after which Powter had to fork over $144,000 in alimony (Musicians. Go figure.). A legal battle with a former partner led to bankruptcy.

In 1997 Powter authored a book called *Sober . . . and Staying That Way*, describing her lifelong struggle with alcoholism (and you thought the only bottle she battled was the one containing Log Cabin Syrup). The last we heard she was teaching aerobics classes in her new hometown of Seattle. We wish her a successful—and calm—future.

RiCHaRD SiMMONS

"Lose weight and celebrate!"

If Jack LaLanne is the father of the American fitness movement, then Richard Simmons is its effeminate bachelor uncle. While LaLanne advocates a strict diet and brutal physical regimen, Simmons offers a touchy-feely, nonjudgmental route to good health that's proved perfect for dumpling-shaped, authority-averse baby boomers. Using his own television show and a slew of infomercials, he's spread his weight loss philosophy around the world—and sold millions of fitness gizmos and videotapes to boot.

Born in New Orleans in 1948, Simmons was the classic pudgy kid who grew up to be a fat adult. He tried diet after diet and even subscribed to *Cosmopolitan* to keep up with the latest weight loss trends. Finally he hit upon a formula any health professional could have given him: instead of dieting and bingeing, simply consume a moderate, balanced diet and start exercising. But Simmons took it one step further. To get a grip on his daily food intake, he created a packet of cards that listed the items and portions from the various food groups he could eat each day. He kept these in a big plastic "wallet," and as he consumed each portion, he transferred the card representing it from one section of the wallet to another. When the cards were gone, he was done eating for the day. Sound familiar, Deal-A-Meal fans?

THE PRODUCT

Various workout videos and exercise products.

STATUS: The classic Deal-A-Meal is gone, but the videos remain.

CLAIMED INNOVATION: The card system took the pain (and math) out of counting calories.

THE UPSIDE: An easy-to-follow calorie control method.

THE DOWNSIDE: Nagging fear that if we follow Simmons's techniques we'll end up looking like him.

AND WHEN HE'S NOT EXERCISING . . .

Simmons collects dolls. He has about 300 at his Los Angeles home, and he even offers a line of reproductions on QVC, through retailers, and on his Web site, richardsimmons.com. Some are so wizened and troll-like that they could be litter-mates to Chuckie or the Zuni fetish doll from *Trilogy of Terror*.

Not surprisingly, Simmons quickly went from porker to pixie. He relocated to Los Angeles and spent two years bouncing from gym to gym, looking for the perfect workout—or rather, the perfect workout for a scrawny little guy who wasn't into high-intensity aerobics or pumping iron. Failing to find what he wanted, he put together his own dance routines at home. In 1974 he took his fitness concepts—but most importantly, his Paul-Lynde-meets-Kathy-Rigby personality—public by opening a Beverly Hills fitness center called Slimmons. Geared to the couch potato set, it's still open today, with its namesake regularly leading classes.

Things didn't really take off until the debut of *The Richard Simmons Show*. The program, which ran for four years during the late '70s and early '80s, fixed the template for Simmons' public persona—a curly-haired, squeaky-voiced sprite in Roller Boogie shorts who led large groups of large people through the lowest sort of low-impact aerobics. Afterward, the Leo Sayer look-alike started rolling out infomercials (the first in 1986 for the now-legendary *Sweatin' to the Oldies* home workout tape), introduced a carefully refined version of Deal-A-Meal, and settled into the same sort of semi-celebrity enjoyed by "luminaries" such as Dr. Joyce Brothers and The Amazing Kreskin.

A recent moneymaker is his *Lose Weight and Celebrate* program, which among other things features three videos set to Broadway show tunes. Another latter success is a calorie-counting system called the FoodMover (an elaboration on the Deal-A-Meal). Simmons himself could be called the Merchandise Mover. He's released more than 30 videos and sold more than 27 million units on QVC. Who among us wouldn't put up with David Letterman's incessant mocking for a small part of such riches?

WHAT'S IN A NAME?

Over the years Simmons has put out tapes with such head-scratching titles as *Dance Your Pants Off, Groovin' in the House,* and *Disco Sweat* (which would have made a great name for an Ohio Players album). Recent releases stick to this high standard, including *Sudor Mucho* (a Spanish-language workout tape), *Platinum Sweat* (a low-impact routine for older people), and *Sit Tight* (a session for the chair-bound).

NOT THAT THERE'S ANYTHING WRONG WITH THAT

Although we feel confident that Mr. Simmons has never furtively leafed through a Victoria's Secret catalog, he's never actually spelled out his sexual orientation. But this hasn't stopped him from having fun with his flamboyant image—particularly during his regular guest appearances on *The Late Show with David Letterman*.

But while the world makes sport of his less-than-macho image, Simmons himself maintains a Sphinxlike (or rather, Seigfried-and-Roy-like) silence. The closest he's come to comment was in a CNN.com interview concerning his autobiography *Still Hungry—After All These Years*. "I have 90 percent of my heart and guts in this book, and I kept 10 percent for me. And the 10 percent is my personal life and death."

SOLOFLEX

"To unlock your body's potential . . ."

Up until the late 1970s, fitness devices were relatively unheard of in the magnificent ASOTV universe. Into that vacant venue strode the Oregon-based athletic equipment company Soloflex, Inc. Because it was one of the first to market a compact, all-purpose "home gym," its ads didn't have to shout down hordes of competitors. The commercials and infomercials could get away with speaking softly and carrying very little shtick.

Compared to today's fitness hard sells, the scripts for the early Soloflex spots read like Shakespeare. They had to be enticing, given the distinctly nonphotogenic nature of the product. The Soloflex home gym (developed by company founder Jerry Wilson) is certainly no looker—just a weight bench with a bar hanging over it. The commercials, however, made it sound like the greatest breakthrough in physical culture since the invention of the jockstrap. As classical music swelled, chiseled male and female models were interposed over da Vinci figure studies. Finally a melodious voice intoned, "To unlock your body's potential, we proudly offer Soloflex."

THE PRODUCT

A home gym that simulates iron-pumping exercises using resistance created by rubber "weight-straps." The more straps you add to the machine, the tougher the workout.

STATUS: On the market.

CLAIMED INNOVATION: Comprehensive home fitness from a single compact device.

THE UPSIDE: One of the more sturdy and elegantly designed home gyms.

THE DOWNSIDE: At $1,195 plus shipping, also one of the more expensive.

To paraphrase the woman from *Jerry Maguire*, they had us at "hello."

Of course it couldn't last. Only a few years after Soloflex's 1978 introduction, competitors took to the airwaves with decidedly more downscale presentations. The brand and its highbrow advertising was pushed aside, like *Playhouse 90* by *McHale's Navy*. Today the company's exercise machines are still manufactured and sold, but to a far smaller audience than in their heyday.

UNAUTHORIZED USE

The basic Soloflex has a "footprint" of only 4 feet by 4 feet. This means it won't take up much space when you abandon your New Year's resolution to "get fit" and start hanging clothes on the crossbar.

POP QUESTION

AREN'T SOLOFLEX AND BOWFLEX MADE BY THE SAME COMPANY?

Ab-solutely not. Far from being stablemates, Bowflex and Soloflex are bitter rivals. When Bowflex took a huge bite out of the home exercise market, some thought the firm did it by swiping a page or two from the Soloflex playbook—including attaching "flex" to their machine's name and hiring their marketing boss from their rival's ranks. Soloflex took offense and filed a $20 million suit alleging illegal use of its trade secrets. Although they admitted no wrongdoing, the Bowflex folks agreed to pay $8 million to settle the case.

TOTALLY USELESS STATISTIC

The official Soloflex Web site states that if all the Soloflex machines ever built were stacked on top of each other, they would reach 900 miles high.

69

Tae-Bo

"I want you to be a conqueror."

Tae-Bo creator Billy Blanks looks like a *Die Hard* extra, but his evangelical flair and relentlessly positive attitude also bring to mind Richard Simmons—albeit a black, bald, buff Richard Simmons who rips his shirt off mid-workout and could crush your skull like a casaba melon.

Tae-Bo (the name combines the first word from Tae Kwon Do and the first two letters of "boxing") broke nationally when infomercials for Blanks's exercise videos started airing in the late '90s. Insomniacs and the unemployed watched in awe as the martial arts master led a group of furiously sweating disciples through his high-energy routine, punctuated by testimonials from celebrity clients such as Shaquille O'Neal, Carmen Electra, and *Playboy* Playmate Shannon Tweed, who apparently didn't fully grasp the meaning of the word "testimonial." "I don't know if I can put it into words," she said of her love for Tae-Bo.

Blanks, on the other hand, can think of lots to say about it. A sign on the wall of his Sherman Oaks exercise studio reads "Walk by Faith, Not by Sight," and he's forever explaining how Tae-Bo improves your spiritual as well as physical state. "You can train and train and train, and even achieve a high degree of physical fitness," he tells his acolytes, "but if you don't develop

THE PRODUCT

High-energy aerobics combining elements of Tae Kwon Do, boxing, and dance. Videos, sold in sets and individually, offer follow-at-home sessions conducted by Billy Blanks.

STATUS: On the market.

CLAIMED INNOVATION: Monster workout utilizing martial arts moves.

THE UPSIDE: Fantastic conditioning tool—if you survive the sessions.

THE DOWNSIDE: You may not survive the sessions. Tae-Bo tapes (usually set to music so relentlessly up-tempo that it sounds like a 33 rpm record played at 45) are tough enough to make a Delta Force member puke.

UNAUTHORIZED USE

Infants seem fascinated by the Tae-Bo Jr. tape—provided the volume is kept low.

discipline, concentration, and dedication, you'll never be truly fit. When you aim high, train hard, and reach your goals, you develop an inner faith that guides your way more securely than your eyes."

Whatever, Grasshopper. The fact that the sweat-soaked participants in his videos sometimes grimace in pain and even fold under the stress makes it clear that Blanks doesn't covet the couch potato market. His approach is 10 percent inspiration, 90 percent perspiration, and it's aimed squarely at folks who, having already attained abs of steel, now want to upgrade to titanium.

POP QUESTION

HOW FIT DO YOU HAVE TO BE TO ATTEMPT THE TAE-BO VIDEO WORKOUTS?

Pretty damn fit. The over-the-head kicks demonstrated in the advanced workouts are impossible for the less than extremely limber. *Muscle & Fitness* magazine rated Tae-Bo the highest calorie-burning workout available, torching 800 calories per hour. Typical aerobics sessions burn about 450 per hour.

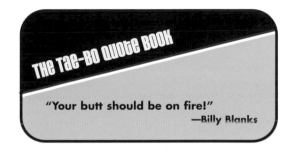

THE TAE-BO QUOTE BOOK

"Your butt should be on fire!"
—Billy Blanks

WHERE ARE THEY NOW?

Having carved out his niche in the celebrity fitness market, Blanks is busily defending it. In part to ward off imitators, he's initiated a teaching program for licensed Tae-Bo instructors. Complete the course to his satisfaction and you earn the right (for a small remuneration, naturally) to use the name "Billy Blanks' Tae-Bo" when promoting classes. These instructors are peppered across North America, from California to North Carolina.

BLANKS BIO

The fourth of 15 kids, Blanks faced poverty, dyslexia, and a hip joint anomaly that made him walk funny. Kids mocked him and coaches considered him a lost cause. At 13, he began taking karate lessons. In 1975 he won the first of five Amateur Athletic Union championships. He went on to become captain of the US Amateur Karate Team.

But he didn't start making the big bucks until he switched from beating people up to beefing them up. While training at home in his basement, he tinkered together a workout regimen combining karate moves and dance music. In 1989 he opened the modestly named Billy Blanks World Training Center in Sherman Oaks, California. Paula Abdul became a client, and soon a long list of Hollywood B-listers (Justine Bateman, Valerie Bertinelli, and Sinbad among them) streamed through the door.

ThighMaster

"Wow, great legs. How'd you get 'em?"

In a genre bursting with oddly named devices designed to roll/knead/glide one's various bodily imperfections into oblivion, the ThighMaster reigns as undisputed champ. But the contraption, which looks like a gigantic, broken paper clip, didn't start out a media darling.

The original version was the brainchild of Swedish chiropractor Anne-Marie Bennstrom, a spiritual guide at a retreat in the Santa Monica Mountains called The Ashram. Bennstrom gave her inspired invention a singularly uninspired name: the V-Bar (hey, no one ever accused the Swedes of being marketing masters, candy fish aside). The system fell into the hands of Josh Reynolds (who gave the world the Mood Ring), who retooled it and anointed it with the marginally catchier name of V-Toner.

Then he brought it to marketer Peter Bieler, and the rest is infomercial history. Early tests of the V-Toner drew a tepid consumer response. But then the bubbly blond from *Three's Company*, Suzanne Somers, was asked to attach her name (and wrap her legs around) the product. The old V-Toner moniker, which made it sound like something you'd pour in a photocopier, was also ditched in favor of the vaguely sexualized ThighMaster.

THE PRODUCT

A butterflied resistance exerciser designed to be squeezed between the thighs.

STATUS: On the market.

CLAIMED INNOVATION: Isolates and tones thighs with an easy-to-do exercise.

THE UPSIDE: If you hammer away at your upper legs with this device, you will see results.

THE DOWNSIDE: The ThighMaster can pop out from between your legs when you get sweaty, a problem of particular concern if your house is populated with small children or pets.

A SOMERS PLACE

Alan Hamal says that when the device was first presented to him and his wife, it was still called the V-Toner and seen primarily as an upper-body workout tool. But then Somers stuck the contraption between her legs, squeezed off a few reps, and demonstrated its utility as a thigh toner—or, as history would remember it, a thigh master. Hamal asserts that, in a frenzy of creative insight, he and his wife also hatched the product's world-beating name.

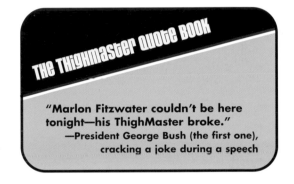
"Wow, great legs. How'd you get 'em?" asked an unseen questioner (actually Somers' husband, Alan Hamel), standing in for all the faceless TV watchers wondering how such admittedly superb gams could be attached to a mere mortal. As the camera continued its slow guide north to Somers' face, America discovered that even though *Three's Company* was long gone, TV's Chrissy Snow hadn't let herself go to pot. And when the nation's female population learned she'd obtained her walnut-cracking thighs using a device they could purchase for the low, low price of $19.95, one could almost hear them stampeding to their phones as fast as their cellulite-spackled legs could carry them.

A phenomenon was born. Within five months of hitting the market, ThighMasters were flying out the door to the tune of 75,000 per week. Of course knockoffs soon flooded the market, but the company (a firm called ThighMaster World Corporation that's now entirely owned by Somers and hubby) triumphed over them in patent litigation. The device became not just a mail-order legend, but also a retail giant proving that it, well, had legs.

THE THIGHMASTER QUOTE BOOK

"Marlon Fitzwater couldn't be here tonight—his ThighMaster broke."
—President George Bush (the first one), cracking a joke during a speech

THIGHMASTER MOVIE APPEARANCES

In *Made in America*, Whoopi Goldberg and Ted Danson are caught making out with the ThighMaster ad running in the background—an image that will live in our nightmares for eternity. In *Forever Young*, the ThighMaster is on the tube when Mel Gibson wakes up from a deep freeze. Rita Rudner and Emma Thompson work out with them in *Peter's Friends*. Damon Wayans does the same in *Major Payne*. It also popped up on *Designing Women* and was a gift that Katie Couric, Joan Lunden, and Paula Zahn gave to Murphy Brown. And that's just the beginning. This device has a better resume than most graduates of *The Actor's Studio*.

An informercial can make a star out of a nobody—witness Susan Powter, Jay "The Juiceman" Kordich, or Ron Popeil. But sometimes it can also feature an actual recognizable face. Whether it's a still-semi-hot celebrity or a down-at-the-heels sitcom refugee one step away from signing autographs at boat shows, they exist to encourage late-night viewers to stop channel grazing and listen up. And the success of many of the products indicates that the tactic works.

Well, sometimes it works. For every runaway hit like ThighMaster, there's a dud like Dolly Parton Cosmetics. For every memorable visit with George Foreman, there's a forgotten half-hour with Lyle Waggoner.

Here, then, are one hundred notable names who helped sell infomercial products. How many of these have sent you running to the phone to "act now"?

#76
Burt Reynolds

#4
Susan Anton

#3
Loni Anderson

#9
Pat Boone

#62
Ricardo Montalban

name	claim to fame	product	name	claim to fame	product
1 Debbie Allen	*Fame* actress, Broadway star, and much-maligned Academy Awards choreographer.	COPA Hair Curl Relaxing System	11 Christie Brinkley	*Sports Illustrated* swimsuit issue fixture, former Billy Joel armpiece.	Total Gym 2000, Total Gym 3000
2 Steve Allen	First *Tonight Show* host; prolific composer of songs you never heard of.	Getting A's the Easy Way home study system	12 Morgan Brittany	*Dallas* star and made-for-TV-movie diva.	Swiss Balance Golden Drops
3 Loni Anderson	Highly coiffed *WKRP in Cincinnati* ensemble member and Burt Reynolds ex.	Loni cosmetics	13 James Brolin	Mr. Streisand.	The Secret of Creating Your Future self-improvement course
4 Susan Anton	Statuesque '70s starlet famous mostly for being famous.	The Power Dome exerciser	14 Dick Butkus	Formerly vicious NFL player turned cuddly all-purpose TV personality.	Qwik-Cool Grill
5 Eddie Arcaro	Five-time Kentucky Derby–winning jockey and one of the top money winners in Thoroughbred racing history.	Bio-Back ergonomic back support	15 David Carradine	Stone-faced star of TV's *Kung Fu*.	*Tai Chi for the Body* and *Tai Chi for the Mind* videos
6 Denise Austin	Host of Denise Austin's *Daily Workout* on the Lifetime cable channel. Resident fitness expert on the *Today* show from 1984 to 1988.	Complete Ten folding exercise equipment	16 Cher	Academy Award–winning actress, drag queen archetype, and former sarcastic half of Sonny and Cher.	Cher Beauty Products
7 Meredith Baxter	On TV: Big sister to Kristy McNichol, mom to Justine Bateman, Bridget to Bernie.	Victoria Jackson Cosmetics	17 Dick Clark	*American Bandstand* host; blooper booster.	You're a Genius and I Can Prove It! learning system
8 Bill Bixby	Eddie's father/The Incredible Hulk's alter ego.	Educate America Today computer and software	18 James Coburn	Academy Award–winning actor often mistaken for Lee Marvin.	*Winning Strategies for Slot Machines* video
9 Pat Boone	White bucks–wearing singer who, inexplicably, was the second most popular singer of the late '50s (behind Elvis).	MDR Fitness Tabs	19 Gary Collins	Generic '70s TV personality often mistaken for Ron Ely.	Select Comfort Air Sleep System
10 Tom Bosley	Tony-Award winner (for *Fiorello!*) and *Happy Days* dad.	Money Makers Live	20 Joan Collins	*Dynasty* alpha bitch.	Bioflora skin care

name	claim to fame	product	name	claim to fame	product
21 Tim Conway	*Carol Burnett Show* regular.	Dorf videos	31 Teri Garr	Professional TV guest star, from *Star Trek* to *Friends*.	Selleca Solution
22 Richard Dysart	*L.A. Law* lawyer.	Sonicare toothbrush	32 Mitch Gaylord	1984 gold medal–winning Olympic gymnast and star of the flop flick *American Anthem*.	Torso Track
23 Erik Estrada	Star of TV's *Chips*.	Natural Premier Supplements' Reduce Fat-Fast	33 Leeza Gibbons	Celebrity softball-question delivery system.	Tony Robbins's Personal Power II, The Driving Force
24 Bob Eubanks	Perennially bemused host of *The Dating Game*.	Prolong Super Lubricants car care kit	34 Kathie Lee Gifford	Tabloid whipping girl.	Mon Amie Cosmetics
25 Linda Evans	Yin to Joan Collins's yang on *Dynasty*.	LegShaper Plus by NordicTrack	35 John Gray, Ph.D.	Whiney-voiced interpersonal relationships guru.	*Men Are from Mars, Women Are from Venus* videotapes
26 Chad Everett	TV doc.	Oncor, a male sexual stimulant	36 Linda Gray	*Dallas* star and *Melrose Place* mom.	The Secret of Creating Your Future motivational series
27 Peggy Flemming	Impossibly well-preserved 1968 Olympic ice-skating champ.	Oral–B Plaque Remover	37 Dick Gregory	Radical comic.	The Bahamian Diet
28 Jane Fonda	Former social revolutionary/workout diva.	T-touch training method for cats and dogs	38 Shelly Hack	Last-quarter, 30-seconds-on-the-clock *Charlie's Angels* substitution.	Theracel Advanced Pro-Cellular System
29 Whitey Ford	New York Yankee, Baseball Hall of Fame inductee, and owner of one of baseball's catchiest names.	Bio-Back ergonomic back support	39 Jack Hanna	The world's premier animal handler, before that crocodile guy came along.	*Talking with Animals* video
30 George Foreman	A fighter so intimidating he actually scared Ali.	George Foreman's Lean Mean Fat-Reducing Grilling Machine, et al.	40 Mel Harris	Sour-faced *thirtysomething* heroine.	Victoria Principal skin-care products

name	claim to fame	product	name	claim to fame	product
Margaux Hemingway 41	Model; Papa's granddaughter.	Tad James self-improvement courses	**Stacy Keach** 51	TV star. Often confused with less-talented brother, James.	The Electronic Cop auto security system
Florence Henderson 42	Brady mom; cooking oil shill.	Expressware Infusion Cooking System	**Angela Lansbury** 52	Broadway legend; *Murder, She Wrote* star.	Beatrix Potter videotapes
Marilu Henner 43	Former *Taxi* star.	Comprehensive Formula Vitamin-mineral supplement	**Robin Leach** 53	Aptly named chronicler of the lifestyles of the rich and famous.	Easy Money coin sorter; Slender Secret weight loss
Charlton Heston 44	Sci-fi and Bible hero; gun advocate.	*Charlton Heston Presents the Bible*	**Judith Light** 54	Better half of *Who's the Boss?* comedy team.	Proactiv Solution acne treatment
Kathy Ireland 45	*Sports Illustrated* swimsuit model; star of sci-fi epic *Alien from L.A.*	Body Shaping Ab Blaster	**Art Linkletter** 55	*Password* host and *Game of Life* endorser.	The Winner's Edge success system
LaToya Jackson 46	Scariest (by a nose) of the musical Jackson clan.	LaToya Jackson's Psychic Friends Network	**Ali MacGraw** 56	Steve McQueen squeeze and *Love Story* star.	Victoria Jackson Cosmetics
Bruce Jenner 47	Olympic decathlon champ and Wheaties eater.	Zero-G Strider	**Lee Majors** 57	TV's *Six Million Dollar Man* and Farrah Fawcett's ex.	Bio-Back ergonomic back support
Davy Jones 48	The littlest Monkee and famed Marsha Brady high school dance date.	*Sixty Greatest Hits of the Sixties* CDs	**Barbara Mandrell** 58	The cute Mandrell sister.	You're a Genius and I Can Prove It! learning system
Quincy Jones 49	Legitimately talented musician and record producer. How did he get here?	Tony Robbins's Personal Power II, The Driving Force	**Donna Mills** 59	*Knott's Landing* vixen.	The Eyes Have It cosmetics
Shirley Jones 50	Mama Partridge.	Everything4Less member shopping service	**Mary Ann Mobley** 60	Jayne Meadows was to Steve Allen as she is to Gary Collins.	Select Comfort Air Sleep System

name	claim to fame	product	name	claim to fame	product
61 Joe Montana	Legendary 49ers QB. Not to be confused with acting stalwart Joe Mantegna.	Contoure Cross Trainer	71 Regis Philbin	Host of *Who Wants to Be a Millionaire*.	*Fabulous '50s* CD collection.
62 Ricardo Montalban	*Fantasy Island* ruler and human star of *Conquest of the Planet of the Apes*.	Nativity Cross (gold cross with stone from the Nativity Cave)	72 Mackenzie Phillips	*One Day at a Time* dropout; Mamas and the Papas fill-in.	Proactiv Solution
63 Pat Morita	Replacement Al on *Happy Days* and star of *Karate Kid* series.	Super Megasize Titanium Drivers	73 Victoria Principal	Good girl on *Dallas*.	The Principal Secret skin-care system
64 Leslie Nielsen	*Poseidon* captain and *Naked Gun* cop.	Bad Golf My Way	74 Sarah Purcell	*Real People* cohost.	Snorefix; Munchables
65 Chuck Norris	TV *Texas Ranger*; post-Eastwood, pre-Van Damme action movie star.	Total Gym 3000	75 Eddie Rabbit	Country singer with lots of old hits that no one can quite remember.	*Academy of Country Music 101 Greatest Country Hits*
66 Judy Norton-Taylor	One of the Walton kids who isn't Richard Thomas.	Dianetics	76 Burt Reynolds	Legendary toupee-wearer and *Smokey and the Bandit* star.	Appears in *Benny Hill Golden Laughter Video Collection*
67 Stuart Pankin	*Not Necessarily the News* star and quintessential wacky sitcom neighbor.	Phase 4 Orthotics	77 Smokey Robinson	Bona fide Motown legend.	*Classic Rhythm and Blues Collection*
68 Dolly Parton	Country singer, theme park inspiration, and frequent *Tonight Show* joke during the Carson era.	Dolly Parton Cosmetics	78 Susan Ruttan	*L.A. Law* cast member without a career afterlife.	Chromatrim Weightloss gum
69 Sandi Patty	Christian singing sensation.	Sandi Patty Animated Bible Series	79 Connie Selleca	'80s eye candy used to spruce up various sitcoms and dramas.	The Selleca Solution
70 Norman Vincent Peale	Positive thinker.	The Power of Positive Thinking self-improvement course	80 Richard Simmons	Elf-like weight loss guru.	Endless stream of weight loss videos and diet systems

name	claim to fame	product	name	claim to fame	product
81 Rex Smith	Singer who gained brief mid-'70s fame as a more masculine alternative to Leif Garrett.	Time-Life music collections	91 Robert Urich	TV trouper most recently seen on the short-lived NBC sitcom *Emeril*.	DeGeorge Home Alliance, save money by building your own home
82 Suzanne Somers	The dumb one on *Three's Company*.	ThighMaster; Torso Track; Butterfly Exerciser	92 Karen Valentine	*Room 222* teacher.	*The Golden Days* CD collection
83 Mark Spitz	Seven-time Olympic gold medalist and dentist.	Prolong Engine Treatment	93 Bob Vila	Home improvement expert and Sears spokesman.	Clench Wrench, Pocket Socket, et al.
84 Jill St. John	Bond girl and only woman ever married to both Jack Jones and Robert Wagner.	Lean Solutions	94 Lyle Waggoner	*Carol Burnett Show* straight man.	OxyWhite Tooth Whitener
85 Kathleen Sullivan	Former ABC News anchor.	Weight Watchers	95 Robert Wagner	Natalie Wood's husband (to anyone over 40). Dr. Evil's sidekick (to everyone else).	Lean Solutions
86 Loretta Swit	Sally Kellerman's *M*A*S*H* replacement.	HydroDent	96 Dionne Warwick	Singer who had trouble finding San Jose.	Psychic Friends Network
87 John Tesh	Former *Entertainment Tonight* host, now some sort of "musician."	*Growing in Love* and *Hidden Keys* romantic advice (both with wife Connie Selleca)	97 Lisa Whelchel	*The Facts of Life* elder student and frequent "Where Are They Now?" subject.	Allen Edwards Hair Care
88 Fran Tarkenton	Minnesota Vikings and New York Giants quarterback; Pro Football Hall of Fame inductee.	Think and Grow Rich	98 Vanna White	Letter turner.	Perfect Smile teeth whitener
89 Lee Trevino	Golf legend.	Tempo Trainer 911 golf speed-measuring device	99 Billy Dee Williams	Colt 45 imbiber; action hero.	Psychic Reader's Network
90 Al Unser	Race car driver and Indianapolis 500 champ.	Prolong Engine Treatment	100 Dweezel Zappa	MTV alumnus; son of Frank Zappa.	*Zappa Music for Pets*, an album featuring animal-friendly tunes

part 4
ENTERTAINMENT
BREAK-
THROUGHS

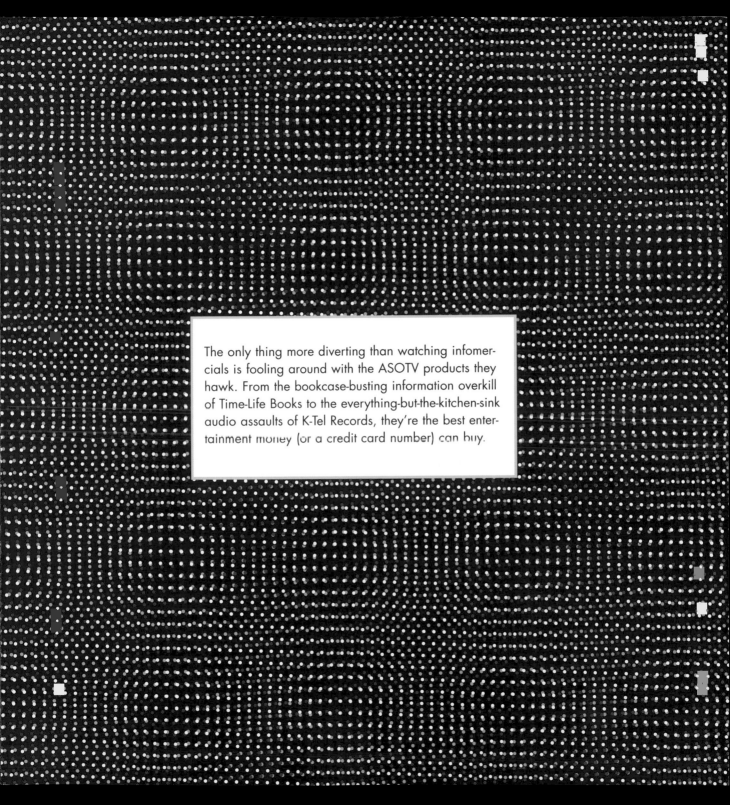

The only thing more diverting than watching infomercials is fooling around with the ASOTV products they hawk. From the bookcase-busting information overkill of Time-Life Books to the everything-but-the-kitchen-sink audio assaults of K-Tel Records, they're the best entertainment money (or a credit card number) can buy.

BLOPENS

"A mind-blowing alternative to fabric paints, transfers, and iron-ons."

Visit any medium-size tourist town and you'll see airbrush artists prowling the backs of T-shirt shops, busily emblazoning articles of clothing with such timeless sentiments as "Camaro Power." Using a tiny paint gun (basically an ink-filled pen attached to a supply of compressed air), the operator lays down graffiti-like swaths of bright color, quickly creating elaborate designs with what seems like minimal effort.

Now parents (after throwing tarps over their furniture) can bring a highly simplified version of this technology home to kids thanks to the Blopen, a brilliant low-tech refinement of the fairly complicated airbrushing system. Gone are the vials of paint, the compressor, and anything else that might require extensive adult supervision. To create the air pressure needed to spray the paint, kids simply wrap their lips around the ends of the disposable Blopens themselves (basically a melding of an ink pen with a kazoo) and blow. Hand these babies over to junior, and out of the mouths of babes come not just gems (and partially digested strained peaches) but works of art.

There's only one real problem with Blopens. Airbrushing looks easy, but in fact it's one of the trickier

THE PRODUCT

Basically a marker encased in a two-part plastic tube. When blown into, the tube forces the ink to spray out the other end, creating an airbrush-like effect on whatever it hits.

STATUS: On the market.

CLAIMED INNOVATION: Kids can enjoy the fun of airbrushing at home!

THE UPSIDE: Hours of fun.

THE DOWNSIDE: Nagging fear that you're going to have the one defective Blopen that sends your pride and joy to the hospital with a case of pink lung.

SPIN-OFFS

Fabric Blopens are also available, as well as a turbo foot pump—perfect for Blopens artists with five-pack-a-day smoking habits.

artistic techniques to master. That's why the Blopen kits come with stencils, so that children can bash out designs—often duckies and doggies, all with the same psychedelic, vaguely Peter Maxx-ish quality about them—without lengthy training.

Although children probably won't produce any Jim Morrison portraits or Keep on Truckin' posters with their Blopens, they should have a good time. The child models on the back of the Blopens box—a group of elementary schoolers with pens in their mouths, looking for all the world like the clientele of some under-21 cigar bar—seem to be. And there's one very important benefit to parents: When your little Matisse has his lips wrapped around a Blopen, it's physically impossible for him to ask for a juice box, complain that his sister is looking at him, or whine about anything else.

safety first

Although placing a paint gun in the mouths of children sounds about as bright as furnishing them with, say, My First Jackhammer, the company's done a good job of addressing most of the obvious concerns arising from such a scheme. The ink, Blopen promotional materials repeatedly assure us, is non-toxic and washes out of almost everything. And the pens are specially designed so that while ink can be blown out, it can't be sucked out. No muss, no fuss, no frantic calls to a poison control hotline. Kids being kids, other near-inevitable crises such as "What should I do if it is sprayed in someone's face?" are extensively covered.

unauthorized use

Blopens create some interesting Easter egg effects, but we don't advise eating the eggs.

the museum of Blopen art

Blopens entertained the children of co-author Lou Harry for more than two hours. Here are just three of their accomplishments (the rest were "blown" onto walls, tabletops, computer screens, and other household valuables).

THE BLOPEN QUOTE BOOK

"For young kids, just remind them to take a break once in a while and to swallow their spittle rather than letting it get into Blopen tube."
—Official Blopen Web site and instruction book

Boxcar Willie

"Rollin' in my sweet baby's arms."

American pop culture is sprinkled liberally with hypocritical xenophobia. We understand completely, for instance, the popularity of Sylvester Stallone, Britney Spears, and *NSYNC on our own shores, but we express condescending bafflement that Jerry Lewis is worshipped as a comic genius in France or that foreigners actually pay to buy David Hasselhoff CDs.

We likewise turned up our red, white, and blue noses at the very idea that Boxcar Willie could become the most popular country music performer in the U.K. Until a commercial hit America's airwaves, that is. Then we, too, fell under the spell of the world's favorite (except, perhaps, for Emmett Kelly) hobo. The ad, touting a two-album set called *King of the Road*, showed a rumpled, overall-clad, two-day-bearded guy who looked like he was just thrown off the Union Pacific by a sledgehammer-wielding Ernest Borgnine. Offering such songs as "Hank and the Hobo," "Move It On Over," and "Rollin' in My Sweet Baby's Arms," the disc launched Willie, if not to Johnny Cash–level stardom, at least to Minnie Pearl–like renown.

Another example (à la Slim Whitman and Zamphir, Master of the Pan Flute) of marketing over matter? Perhaps. A bold packaging move that would eventually leave the world vulnerable to Ann Murray greatest hits

THE PRODUCT

Country-western music compilation.

STATUS: Off the market.

CLAIMED INNOVATION: Authentic but mass-appeal country crooning.

UPSIDE: Better than half the *Hee-Haw* cast.

DOWNSIDE: He's no Waylon, Willie, or Hank.

DEATH OF A HOBO

The flags flew at half-staff all over Branson when Willie moseyed off into the afterlife in 1999 at age 67. On the first anniversary of his death, he was honored by Red Oak, Texas, with The Boxcar Willie Memorial Overpass. Two of the man's guitar picks were inserted into one of the bridge's concrete walls.

collections? Absolutely. Nevertheless, Willie developed a following and was taken seriously by those who matter in country music—the gatekeepers of the Grand Ole Opry. In 1981, at the invitation of Roy Acuff, Willie joined the Opry, and that same year, he was named "Most Promising Male Country Singer" by Nashville's *Music City News*. He was 50 years old.

Willie knew how to handle his success. After 10 years of nearly nonstop touring, he became one of the first stars to stake a claim on Branson, Missouri, where he founded the Boxcar Willie Theatre (as well as the Boxcar Willie Museum and Boxcar Willie Motel). There he performed six shows a week, nine months a year, before losing a battle with leukemia in 1999.

THE BOXCAR WILLIE QUOTE BOOK

"I remember a comment Boxcar Willie made years ago. He was selling, like, a million records on television. A Columbia Records guy said, 'We want to sign you.' And Boxcar goes, 'Well, why would I want to do that?'"
—Musician John Hyatt, explaining to the Associated Press why he doesn't feel the need to have a major record deal

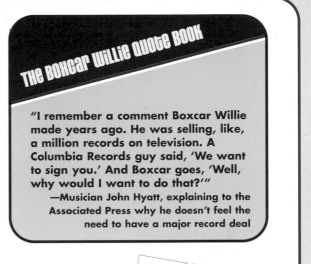

BOXCAR BACKGROUND

Born Lecil Travis Martin in Sterret, Texas, Willie sang in local shows before putting his music career on hold to join the U.S. Air Force in 1949. He trained on the B-36 bomber and, during the Korean War, served as flight engineer on B-29s.

Throughout his 22 years in the military, Willie played in a series of bands and enjoyed modest success in Nashville. He even won on *The Gong Show* in 1977. Then came the first in a series of improbable breaks. Filling in for an ailing George Jones at a club, he was noticed by a Scottish booking agent who landed him a spot at the International Country Music Festival at Wembly Stadium and a record deal with MCA Nashville. Four years of huge success in Europe ensued, followed by the *King of the Road* commercial that brought him stateside.

WHAT'S IN A NAME?

Legend has it that Willie's childhood home sat only six feet away from the railroad tracks where his father worked as a section hand. But while his early years were spent trainspotting, his signature nickname wasn't born until some time in the '50s when he was stuck at a railroad crossing. A man sitting in a passing boxcar looked so much like his boom operator, Willie Wilson, that the man-who-would-be-BW thought "There goes Willie." Seizing the momentary inspiration, he pulled off the road and began to write a song called "Boxcar Willie." Eventually he adopted the name for himself.

CHARLTON HESTON PRESENTS THE BIBLE

"I'm not a priest or a scholar. I'm an actor."

Although Heston is narrator and host of this home video collection, he seems to fear he's bitten off more than he can chew. At the beginning of one of the tapes he states with admirable humility, "I'm Charlton Heston. I'm not a priest or a scholar. I'm an actor." Apparently he feels the need to state, right up front, that his contribution to this project is strictly non-prophet.

He may not be a priest or scholar, but he makes a fair-to-middling tour guide during this four-tape journey to the Bible's most important settings—a sort of Mobil Guide to the Holy Land. Heston traipses over hallowed ground while offering historical insight and reading from the Good Book. Although a noted conservative, Heston goes to great lengths to state that the tapes concern the stories of the Bible, not the literal truth of this or that smoting incident. The prophets, he carefully hedges, preached God's word "as they perceived it."

THE PRODUCT

A four-video collection of Bible stories and history featuring Charlton Heston.

STATUS: On the market.

CLAIMED INNOVATION: ". . . recaptures all the passion, the power, the drama, and the sheer beauty those first storytellers passed on to us . . ."

THE UPSIDE: A wealth of interesting detail.

THE DOWNSIDE: Only people who came of age in the '50s still think of Heston as "Mr. Bible." To those born later he's the sneering anti-hero from *Soylent Green* and *Planet of the Apes*. To those born after the '70s, he's the gun guy.

Heston starts with a strong premise: that before the written word, the prime source of information was storytelling. And so he continues that tradition, emphasizing storytelling over doctrine. Genesis gets one tape, as does Moses. Jesus, always hogging the spotlight, gets two. Of course, most storytellers of millennia past didn't wear black handkerchiefs around their necks or sport safari clothes that look like Banana Republic clearance-sale finds. Equally annoying are the moments when Heston—often seen tooling around in a Jeep like an aging Indiana Jones—starts doing "voices." His interpretation of the Garden of Eden's serpent sounds suspiciously like the evil bridge guardian in *Monty Python and the Holy Grail*.

The series is co-executive produced by Heston's son Fraser, who can't seem to get work without riding Dad's coattails (four of the five flicks on his IMDB.com filmography feature Pop). Directing chores on this epic went to Tony Westman who, eight years later, would serve as cinematographer for the cable TV movie *Halloweentown II: Kalabar's Revenge*. A step up? Only Jack Valenti knows for sure.

CHARLTON HESTON IN ... THE BIBLE

Best known biblically for his performance as Moses in 1956's *The Ten Commandments*, Heston also played John the Baptist in *The Greatest Story Ever Told* and the title character in the quasi-scriptural *Ben Hur*. Although he continues to work steadily in Hollywood, he hasn't had a big part in an A-list picture since 1974's *Earthquake*.

SPIN-OFFS

Watched all four tapes and still can't get enough Heston? Then order *Charlton Heston Presents The Bible Behind the Scenes*, featuring "never-before-seen documentary footage" that takes viewers "behind the scenes to see firsthand how this epic multinational production was filmed."

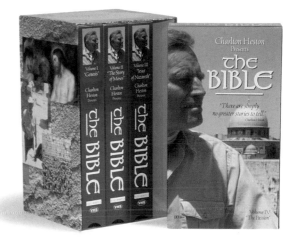

THE BIBLE JR.

The hestonbible.com Web site recently offered a special deal for the kiddies: Purchasers of the 13-video *Greatest Heroes and Legends of The Bible* collection also got four free Bible Activity Pads and a box of "Jesus Loves You" Crayons.

IF WE RULED THE WORLD ...

GT Direct Infomercials, marketers of the *Charlton Heston Presents The Bible* videos, would allow its other celebrity clients to contribute to the series. The result? *Richard Simmons Presents the Bhagavad Gita*.

CHia Pet

"Cha-Cha-Cha-Chia!"

Every holiday season the Vast Wasteland echoes with the electronic mating call of one of the world's most enduring ASOTV products. Pay attention to the commercial breaks during *Cheers* reruns and you'll undoubtedly hear—over and over—the same distinctive cry: "Cha-cha-cha-Chia!"

Yes, they're Chia Pets, the little terra-cotta statues that infest drugstores and middlebrow retail outlets from October to December. For the better part of three decades, they've held an unassailable spot in the American consciousness, thanks mostly to their Chia daddy, Joseph Pedott, president of the San Francisco–based advertising and marketing firm Joseph Enterprises.

Actually he's more like their Chia stepdaddy. Pedott didn't think of the original idea—far from it. But it was Pedott who transformed this innocuous trifle into a phenomenon.

The magic began in the early '70s when he heard that a Chicago-based industrial concern was offering Chias in a small number of markets. "It was selling well, but the importer was losing a lot of money," Pedott recalls. "So I offered to buy it from them. A year later the owner called me and asked if the offer was still good."

THE PRODUCT

Terra-cotta statues that grow chia "hair."

STATUS: On the market.

CLAIMED INNOVATION: Gardening fun.

THE UPSIDE: For only $15 to $16 you get a Chia Pet and enough seeds for three growth cycles.

THE DOWNSIDE: Chia "hair" has the shelf life of sea monkeys—the plants start to fade after four weeks.

POP QUESTION

SO CAN YOU EAT THE CHIA PLANTS?

The instructions say you shouldn't, but . . . yeah. *Salvia columbariae* was popular among the Aztecs, who ground the seeds for flour and pressed them for oil. The sprouts are also edible and can occasionally be found in health food stores. Joseph Enterprises has never sought FDA approval for its pets, but if you're simply starving, have at it. However, you'd have to be in an awfully special place to look at your Chia Pet and think, "Yum!"

It was. Joseph Enterprises acquired a product whose most valuable feature turned out to be its goofy moniker. "Chia" is the common name for *Salvia columbariae*, the seeds of which produce the statues' green "hair." Pedott kept only the title and the basic idea. "We threw away everything but the name, then built from the bottom up with a new product," he says.

The result is a hollow terra-cotta figure that's first soaked in water, placed in a clear plastic drip tray, then plastered with pre-moistened Chia seeds. Just water this assemblage regularly and within a week or two, presto! You've got a hollow terra-cotta figure with vegetation all over it. The process is about as dramatic as waiting for a pot of water to boil, yet for some reason consumers can't get enough.

In this age of instant gratification, it's nice to see a popular TV product that requires its owner to display almost Zen-like patience and calm. Chia Pets don't promise rock-hard abs, overnight riches, or luck in love. Instead, if you follow instructions, you reap the reward of watching a bunch of seedlings sprout. Buddha would be proud.

UNAUTHORIZED USE

No, Cheech and Chong fans, turning your Chia Pet into a Pot Head by sprinkling it with marijuana seeds won't work. They're too big—or so "a friend" tells us. But the figurines readily accommodate other herbs, including basil, alfalfa, marjoram, and thyme.

REASON TO FEAR FOR OUR PUBLIC EDUCATION SYSTEM

Should the process of slathering wet seeds on a piece of clay prove too daunting, you can contact Joseph Enterprises' Chia Hotline at (888) 999-CHIA for assistance. Seriously.

KNOCKOFFS

Over the years various Chia-like rip-offs have hit the market, most of them satirical takes on the original creatures and none of them associated with Joseph Enterprises. The clones include a bust of Grateful Dead leader Jerry Garcia, plus a replica of human genitalia with sprouts standing in for pubic hair.

SEARCHING FOR CHIA

The pets are available only during the holiday season, because it takes months to stockpile enough of the handmade clay figures (created via a multi-day shaping, drying, kiln firing, and finishing process) to satisfy demand. Although Chia Pet boxes state that their contents are "handmade by artisans using techniques passed down from the Indians of ancient Mexico," the people making today's models all reside in China.

Those workers patiently turn out some 20 different Chia designs, including the ever-popular bunny, kitten, and cow, along with more recent oddities such as the Chia Guy (a comical bust that, sans chia sprouts, resembles a severely inebriated NBA coach Pat Riley) and Chia Elmer Fudd. There's even a bust of Mr. T.

THE Clapper

"Clap on, clap off!"

Everything about The Clapper, from its inane commercials to its grating jingle ("Clap on, clap off, clap on, clap off—The Clapper!") brands it as kitsch of the lowest order. Yet it enthralls consumers so thoroughly that tens of thousands of the devices fly off store shelves each year. Even the advertising boasts the can't-look-away allure of a car wreck.

The Clapper first appeared in the mid-'70s and proved an instant hit. This early model was larger and more primitive than the ones sold today, but the basic function was the same then as now. Clap twice with a 1 to 1 ½-second pause between beats and The Clapper turns on a TV, light, radio, or other appliance. Clap three times and it does the same for a second item. Repeat the process and it deactivates one or both, depending on the number of claps.

The size of the unit shrank as its capabilities grew. The 21st-century Clapper includes a dial to adjust its sound sensitivity and lights that flash when it registers claps. It can even perform as a rudimentary burglar alarm, activating at the slightest commotion.

The device is only available in retail outlets during the holiday season (October through December), but it can still be ordered year-round on the Web from

THE PRODUCT

A sound-activated switch into which two appliances can be plugged, then turned on and off by clapping.

STATUS: On the market.

CLAIMED INNOVATION: Hands-free lighting for everyone!

THE UPSIDE: It really works.

THE DOWNSIDE: The "Clap on, clap off!" commercial haunts the mind like a Vietnam flashback.

Joseph Enterprises. Be advised that it sometimes takes a few tries before adults acquire the proper clapping rhythm to make it respond (interestingly, pets and children seem to pick it up right away, whether you want them to or not). If you get into real trouble, you can swallow your pride and call the Clapper Help Desk at (800) 557-5856 for assistance.

POP QUESTION

WHAT STOPS THE CLAPPER FROM BEING ACTIVATED BY NOISES OTHER THAN CLAPPING?

Absolutely nothing—which is why you should never hook it to, say, a toaster or coffeemaker. Also, think twice before hooking one to a TV. Cheer or shout during an exciting sporting event and you may inadvertently shut off the tube.

UNAUTHORIZED USES

Deaf people position Clappers near their phones so they'll know when they ring, and dogs have been trained to turn lights on and off by barking. "One guy [activated his clapper] by smacking his wife on the buttocks two times," developer Joseph Pedott says. "I didn't think that was exactly in good taste."

THE ULTIMATE ENDORSEMENT

In his book *The Salesman of the Century*, Ron Popeil names The Clapper as the one device he wishes he invented. He refuses to buy one because "It would keep reminding me of something I should have made."

Captain Clapper

The world can thank Joseph Pedott, president of the San Francisco–based advertising and marketing firm Joseph Enterprises (and the brains behind another ASOTV favorite, the Chia Pet) for this innovation. Pedott entered the world of household gadgetry back in the '70s, when his firm was hired to promote a sound-activated switch called The Great American Turn On. The idea was pure gold, but there was a problem: The Great American Turn On wouldn't turn on. "It didn't work," Pedott says. "Eventually the government put the creator out of business. But the concept was sound, so I spent a couple of years developing the idea. That's how it started."

THE DEAN MARTIN CELEBRITY ROASTS

"This week's man of the hour ..."

Charlton Heston may visit the Holy Land in his video-tape series (see page 86), but a trip into equally exotic and unfamiliar territory can be had by TV shoppers who enter the world of the Dean Martin Celebrity Roast.

This videotape library transports viewers into another comedic time—an era peopled by high-profile funny-men such as Bob Hope, George Burns, and Hubert Humphrey (well, at least his name was funny). It was a format uniquely suited for the one-of-a-kind skills of stammering Foster Brooks, pocketbook-wielding Ruth Buzzi, and rubber-faced Charlie Callas.

The roasting ritual evolved from *The Dean Martin Show*, a launched-in-1965 variety series built around the laid-back, 100-proof talents of the "Everybody Loves Somebody" crooner and Jerry Lewis straight man. By the show's ninth season it was running out of steam, with Dean and his Golddiggers (read, heavily coifed chickie babes) looking increasingly anachronistic. Fighting entropy, Martin's producer, Greg Garrison, gave over a portion of each show to a segment featuring Dean presiding over the heckling of a high-profile celeb.

THE PRODUCT

A videotape series in which celebs major and minor insult and/or are insulted in front of a live audience under the watchful eye (or, rather, the drooping eyelids) of Dean Martin.

STATUS: On the market.

CLAIMED INNOVATION: Brought Friars Club–style roasting to the masses.

THE UPSIDE: Most of the guests seem to be having a good time.

THE DOWNSIDE: The still-relevant jokes are few and far between.

UNAUTHORIZED USE

Grandpa getting on your nerves? Pop Dean in the VCR. It has the same effect on oldsters that *Sesame Street* has on preschoolers.

Even after the variety series folded, the roasts remained, migrating from Hollywood to their true spiritual home, Las Vegas. Over the years Lucille Ball, Jackie Gleason, Sammy Davis, Jr., George Burns, Muhammad Ali, Jimmy Stewart, and Frank Sinatra (and, during lesser weeks, Betty White, Mr. T, Joan Collins, and Valerie Harper) took turns to the left of the podium. Other names, including Orson Welles, Dom DeLuise, Phyllis Diller, and LaWanda Page, took cheap shots at the guests of honor via carefully scripted jokes. Only the magical triad of Don Rickles, Nipsey Russell, and Jonathan Winters were allowed to improvise.

Not since Joseph Stalin told after-dinner jokes has third-rate humor been greeted with so much dais-pounding, head-shaking, drink-spilling, convulsive laughter. Never have so many celebs (even Michael Landon) blithely smoked in public, and never—except perhaps for *The Battle of the Network Stars* or the Democratic National Convention—have so many Hollywood denizens seemed so far out of their element.

POP QUESTION

HOW DATED ARE THESE TAPES?

To find out, ask a Gen Xer to tell you (1) the name of the comic who built his routines around the line, "never had a dinner"; (2) the title of Angie Dickinson's TV series; or (3) the specific reason Connie Stevens was ever considered a celebrity. (The answers are Red Buttons; *Police Woman*, and "We don't have a clue either," respectively.)

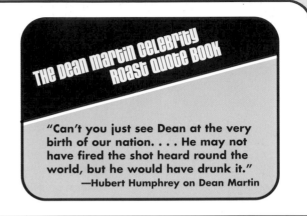

THE DEAN MARTIN CELEBRITY ROAST QUOTE BOOK

"Can't you just see Dean at the very birth of our nation. . . . He may not have fired the shot heard round the world, but he would have drunk it."
—Hubert Humphrey on Dean Martin

REASONS WHY POLITICAL CORRECTNESS MAYBE ISN'T SUCH A BAD IDEA

Roast target Johnny Carson, given the customary opportunity to shoot back at the end of his pillorying, says that Redd Foxx's ancestors "originated the idea of roasting people." And on another tape, Red Buttons, explaining why Shirley Temple Black never got a dinner, jokes, "As ambassador to Ghana, she could *be* the dinner."

THE AWFUL TRUTH

According to TV producer Lee Hale's book, *Backstage at the Dean Martin Show*, "(Dean) wasn't interested in who we roasted, who was on the dais, or when we wanted to tape. We knew he'd show up because he probably had nothing else to do. He faded into the background, becoming just a figurehead whose name we simply used over the title." According to Hale, during the last few roasts the editors had to dig back into the archives to find usable reaction shots of their star.

Dorf Videos

"There's a little Dorf in all of us."

When VCRs first made their way into homes, conventional thinkers saw them merely as an aftermarket for Hollywood films and a new way for home moviemakers to bore their friends. Few, besides pornographers, saw them as a potential gold mine for original programming.

Then came media visionary Tim Conway. *The Carol Burnett Show/Apple Dumpling Gang* alumnus somehow realized that VCR technology fascinated the general public in much the same way basic television mesmerized viewers in the '50s. Back then people would spend hours watching test patterns. Perhaps, just perhaps, consumers would look just as fondly upon quicky straight-to-video productions.

Thus the Dorf videos were born.

Conway and the gang at video house Parvenu Productions, Inc., created their own form of hybrid media—the lower-than-low-budget, character-driven, longer-than-a-cartoon, shorter-than-a-movie videotaped program. As unique as David Lynch movies, Jackson Pollack paintings, and Bazooka Joe comics, the Dorf Video series deftly sidesteps what we normally think of as "humor" (i.e., something that is "funny") and offers something else. What they strive for seems akin

THE PRODUCT

Comedy videotapes.

STATUS: On the market.

CLAIMED INNOVATION: Direct-to-video humor.

THE UPSIDE: Good to see that Conway, who seems like a really nice guy, is keeping busy.

THE DOWNSIDE: This ain't no *Carol Burnett Show*.

to a jazz riff—specifically, the marijuana-influenced jazz riff. Like Coltrane and Diz, Conway takes a familiar melody (say, the fishing joke) and offers variation after off-kilter variation until the viewer drifts into an altered state of consciousness.

Conway's *deus ex machina* is Dorf, a mustached short fellow (he achieves the effect by putting shoes on his knees) with something akin to a German accent. Like Mel Brooks but unlike nearly every eastern European citizen over the age of 60, Conway finds humor in short Germans with mustaches.

Dorf's role is to survive the travails dealt him by an uncaring universe. Consider *Dorf Goes Fishing*, a 45-minute tape that sold more than 500,000 copies and made the *Billboard* Top 40. It could more accurately be called *Dorf Repeatedly Injures Himself with Fishing Tackle*. Something similar could be said of *Dorf and the First Games on Mount Olympus*, where, participating in the first Olympics, he manages to explore all of the possible hazards inherent in the javelin and discus.

At press time the most recent addition was *Dorf da Bingo King*, which attempts to mine bingo halls for laughs. Promotional material claims it will have "players everywhere falling out of their 'lucky seats' with laughter."

Maybe, maybe not. It's doubtless that someone could write a doctoral thesis on the Dorf phenomena. If you'd like to do the research, Bowling Green University would be a good place to start. Mr. Conway donated his personal papers to the school's Popular Culture Library.

POP QUESTION

WHICH CAME FIRST, TIM CONWAY OR HARVEY KORMAN?

Korman was born in 1927, Conway in 1933. In professional terms, Conway was first to make a name for himself when he costarred on TV's *McHale's Navy*. Although Korman enjoyed some success voicing The Great Gazoo on *The Flintstones* in 1965, he didn't become a household name until landing a spot on *The Carol Burnett Show* in 1967. Conway joined the cast in 1975. Ironically, the two also paired up in a Dorf-like "comedy hunting video" called *Tim and Harvey in the Great Outdoors*.

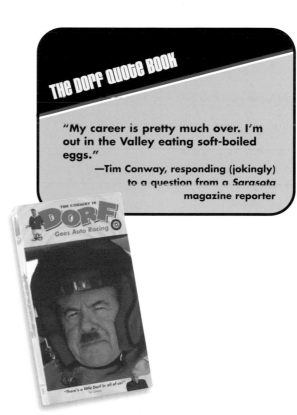

THE DORF QUOTE BOOK

"My career is pretty much over. I'm out in the Valley eating soft-boiled eggs."

—Tim Conway, responding (jokingly) to a question from a *Sarasota* magazine reporter

GiRLS GONE WiLD

"Uncensored and beyond!"

There are lessons to be learned everywhere in this world. If you happen to have seen a *Girls Gone Wild* production, or even caught the oh-so-subtle cable TV ads, you know that the lesson is "Lock up your daughters."

If you don't have daughters, the lesson is still "Lock up your daughters." Unless, of course, you're a college-age guy with an overactive libido. In that case, the lesson is: "Go south for spring break, young man."

"Get educated" screams the cover of the two-volume DVD set *College Girls Exposed* and *Sexy Sorority Sweethearts*. What we learn is that the only thing required to entice a young woman into removing her top is a set of Mardi Gras beads and a little pleading. And it doesn't hurt that the girls being approached seem to have drunk their weight in alcohol. With minimal cinematography (basically, one AV kid with a handheld video), no niceties such as music (except in the credit-less credit sequence), and editing as clunky as the footage of your last Disney World vacation, each recording relentlessly plows forward. Women on the street are asked to bare all. Women on the beach are asked to bare all. Women on hotel balconies are asked to bare all. (Note that just about every scene occurs in a public place, reducing the

THE PRODUCT

A series of videotapes consisting largely of women exposing themselves.

STATUS: On the market.

CLAIMED INNOVATION: Endless parade of drunk college-educated exhibitionists.

THE UPSIDE: Truth in advertising. The tapes are simply longer, uncensored versions of the commercials.

THE DOWNSIDE: The tapes somehow manage to make looking at naked women dull.

need for pesky "releases" from the subjects.) Granted, pornographic cinema always contains a certain element of *vérité*, but this is ridiculous.

Is there a positive side to this? Well, the anonymous *Girls Gone Wild* filmmakers do show themselves to be equal opportunity perverts. They beg women regardless of race, creed, or whether they conform to mainstream standards of physical beauty. While there is an occasional girl-next-door in the pack, many wouldn't stand out in a Ricki Lake audience. Which leads us to the obvious question: How do the *GGW* people know these women are, in fact, college students, much less sorority sweethearts?

Better that they aren't. We pity the poor senior who returns from spring break to find her featured *GGW* performance playing on every VCR on campus.

THE BETTER PART OF VALOR

Girls Gone Wild videos and DVDs are shipped in a brown box with a discreet white label. Those paying by credit card will see a charge to MRA Video.

THE GIRLS GONE WILD QUOTE BOOK

". . . frontal, dorsal and always drunkal . . ."
— *Entertainment Weekly* critic Josh Wolk, describing the flashing montages on a *GGW* tape

SPIN-OFFS

Do you own your own video camera? Do you hang out with drunk women? Then order the *Girls Gone Wild* Crew T-shirt. Think of it as the *GGW* home game.

GIRL-OF-THE-MONTH CLUB

Think *College Girls Exposed* is just stupid fun? Wait until you sign on to receive a new *Girls Gone Wild* title each month to "preview." While the original *GGW* offerings don't reveal much more than your average episode of *Red Shoe Diaries*, these "Totally Exposed" tapes, while still using amateur talent, are hard-core efforts featuring close-ups that would make Larry Flint blush.

K-Tel Records

"22 original hits by the original artists!"

For four decades K-Tel Records was the worldwide leader in compilation music discs—"all hits" albums for people who wanted Top 40 tunes and nothing but. Ever buy a record because you liked a particular song, only to find yourself wading through 60 minutes of power ballads, guitar solos, and instrumentals just to reach that lone diamond in the dirt? If so, K-Tel was for you. Like a sonic version of The Juiceman (page 22), it wrung out all the extraneous material and gave customers nothing but the good stuff—in no particular order.

Characterized in its prime by a relentless insistence that its discs contained "original hits/original stars," the company specialized in two types of offerings. The first was no-rhyme-or-reason compendiums of the previous year's Top 40 hits—how else to explain one thoroughly typical menagerie called *Believe in Music*, featuring an oil-and-vinegar mix that included Dr. Hook and the Medicine Show's "Sylvia's Mother," The O'Jays's "Back Stabbers," and Cher's "Gypsies, Tramps and Thieves"?

The other common K-Tel product was collections of single-artist or single-band hits (Gordon Lightfoot and The Marshall Tucker Band, to name two) that usually hit store shelves long after a true greatest hits collection had been released by the artist's label.

THE PRODUCT

Recording compilations.

STATUS: Some still on the market.

CLAIMED INNOVATION: All hits. No filler.

THE UPSIDE: There were a lot of hits.

THE DOWNSIDE: Getting caught with a K-Tel disc in your collection could destroy a relationship before it began.

K-TEL: BEYOND THE MUSIC

K-Tel tried to venture into the larger world of ASOTV merchandise. This led to such now-forgotten products as the K-Tel Micro Roast, The Original K-Tel Knitter, the K-Tel Quick Chill Ice Cream Maker, and the K-Tel Micro-Chip Microwave Potato Chip Maker.

Always trying to incorporate the lingo of those crazy kids, the compilations sported such "groovy" titles as *Super Bad*, *Dynamite*, and *Disco Mania*. But K-Tel was like a 300-pound rock-concert roadie; it associated with cool things but was never itself cool. Still, it served its purpose—keeping us from purchasing an entire album of, say, Captain and Tennille tunes just to get "Muskrat Love." And besides, who among us could resist a record company brazen enough to offer The DeFranco Family's "Save the Last Dance for Me," Kool and the Gang's "Hollywood Swinging," and Sister Janet Mead's "The Lord's Prayer" all on the same disc?

Though most people think the company died out along with vinyl records, K-Tel survived into the Internet age. It tried selling its wares on the Web, offering would-be producers the chance to build their own compilations from the nearly 5,000 songs in the company's collection. But such brazen, Napster-esque gimmicks weren't enough to keep it going. Major labels, smelling cash, horned in on the "all hits" business. Sony and Columbia Records' *Now That's What I Call Music* compilation was climbing the charts just as K-Tel, in March of 2001, filed for bankruptcy. *Fortune* magazine called it, without apologies to Don McLean or Buddy Holly, "The day the music died."

Pop Question

WHAT DOES K-TEL MEAN?

K-Tel stands for Kevis Television, after founder Philip Kevis, who got things spinning in 1962 (circa "Peppermint Twist")—although he didn't start marketing albums until 1968 (circa "Abraham, Martin and John"). The company went public in 1971 (circa "Maggie May") and bankrupt in 1984 (circa "Owner of a Lonely Heart"). It rebuilt and chugged along steadily until 1998 (circa "My Heart Will Go On"), when the announcement of a Web site sent the stock rocketing. It didn't stay up there for long. In 2001 (circa "Bye, Bye, Bye"), after being booted off the NASDAQ, it closed its US distribution subsidiary.

The Bottom of a Pretty Deep Barrel

If we have to pick the most pathetic of K-Tel offerings, we'll go with *Kids Incorporated*, a "no original stars" 1984 disc featuring such "chart-topping hits" as "Let's Hear It for the Boy," "Against All Odds (Take a Look at Me Now)," and "I'm So Excited"—all sung by children.

Marvin's Magic Drawing Board

THE MAGIC DRAWING BOARD

"Create endless amazing pictures and effects!"

In the beginning there was Etch A Sketch. This brilliantly designed, TV-like box was basically a mess-free art kit. Anyone with minimal motor skills could create designs simply by turning a couple of knobs. Granted, it was nearly impossible to make anything but squares—as anyone who ever spent a rainy afternoon trying to execute a halfway recognizable circle can attest—but the point wasn't to do a masterpiece. It was to pass some time engaged in a quiet, non-messy endeavor (or at least that's how parents saw it). If you weren't pleased, all you had to do was turn the entire works upside down and shake. If only the typical laptop were so user-friendly.

Inventors have tried for decades to improve on the Etch A Sketch concept. Magna Doodle did a respectable job. Wooly Willy (the guy with the magnetic hair) had his champions. But all paled before the red, twin-dialed original. Then along came the latest contender, Marvin's Magic Drawing Board.

The Etch has nothing to worry about.

THE PRODUCT

An erasable, ink-covered drawing board.

STATUS: On the market.

CLAIMED INNOVATION: Allows children to create no-mess artistic masterpieces.

THE UPSIDE: Initial fascination.

THE DOWNSIDE: Endless frustration.

THE AGE OF MAGIC

The TV ad says Marvin is "perfect for any age"—although the packaging limits this range to ages 4 to 104. But while we've seen four-year-olds work themselves into a fever pitch of frustration with the device, we didn't have the heart to try for the same effect with arthritic centenarians.

Marvin's looks, at first glance, like a minimalist painting—nothing but framed blackness. But scrawl on it with the appallingly named "multipoint drawing tool" (which any self-respecting five-year-old will lose in a matter of minutes) and you start to see multicolored lines. It seems that under the board's plastic cover resides a reservoir of petroleum-like goo. Scratching the surface with the tool pushes the goo aside, revealing swaths of permanent color on the hard surface below.

If you buy into Marvin's commercials, this process is a passport to hours of mess-free artistic fun. If only it were so. Fact is, the black substance is difficult to move with the "multipoint drawing tool" and tends to ooze back into previously cleared spaces.

Erasing is even more frustrating. Instead of shaking your failed efforts into oblivion, the Marvin board requires users to smear the black stuff around. On TV this operation looks as easy as icing a cupcake. "A few quick swipes and you're ready to create another masterpiece," says the announcer over a frenetic, Benny Hill–caliber soundtrack. Fat chance. Trying to coat the whole board with black goo is like trying to cover a king-size bed with a queen-size sheet.

Still, never let it be said that frustration can't, in its own bitter, disappointing way, be fascinating. After all, how many of the millions of people who purchased Rubik's Cubes actually solved them? Maybe that's what's helped Marvin and his spin-offs (Magic Made Easy, 3-D Art Set, and Ultimate Pen Set) generate more than $60 million in sales.

EVERYBODY'S AN ART CRITIC

At amazon.com, consumers visiting the Marvin's Magic Drawing Board page took time out of their busy lives to post such comments as "one of the least used toys I've ever purchased," "save your money and buy lots of crayons, markers and paper," and "pass on this toy and get a Magna Doodle." The reviews at epinions.com were equally brutal. "Sorry, no magic here," says one. "The worst toy I ever purchased," says another. "Marvin makes kids cry," chimes in yet another. This litany of disappointment was tempered by one lone supporter who gave Marvin four stars and stated that there's a "learning curve" involved.

THE QVC CONNECTION

Marvin's Magic Drawing Board is brought to you by Q Direct, the direct marketing division of the television shopping network QVC.

IT'S A MARV WORLD AFTER ALL

The back of Marvin's box offers a guide to saying the product's name in other languages. That should come in handy if the customer service agent you return it to doesn't speak English. You could say, "*Die Zaubermaltafel* is certainly no Etch A Sketch" (German); or "I lost the multipoint drawing tool for *L'Ardoise Magique*" (French); or "*El Tablero de Dibujo Magico* is very frustrating indeed." (Spanish).

Mr. Microphone

"Hey good lookin', we'll be back to pick you up later!"

Hear those words and the commercial that inspired them unspools in your mind, as familiar and painful as the Zapruder film. Two guys and a girl roll down the street in a '70s-era convertible. As they pass, the curly-haired kid riding shotgun turns and . . . look out, he's got a microphone!

This is how America was introduced to one of the oddest gadgets ever to spring from the fertile mind of Ron Popeil. Sandwiched into his product lineup somewhere between The Ronco Smokeless Ashtray and the Ronco Bottle and Jar Cutter, Mr. Microphone was that rare Popeil brainchild that didn't seem to have a bona fide use. You could, if you really tried, envision a housewife finding a truly practical purpose for, say, the Miracle Broom, or an aspiring country star getting his money's worth from The Ronco Rhinestone and Stud Setter (see page 32). But Mr. Microphone filled no such need.

Unless, of course, you felt the need to embarrass yourself.

THE PRODUCT

An **AM** radio transmitter hiding inside a microphone case. Speak into the mic and your voice issues from the closest (turned on) radio.

STATUS: Off the market.

CLAIMED INNOVATION: Your voice could now be heard on the radio.

THE UPSIDE: Your voice could, in fact, be heard on the radio.

THE DOWNSIDE: It was still your voice.

UNINTENDED LEGACY

Half the world's deejays, music studio grunts, and rock concert sound men are nicknamed Mr. Microphone.

Apparently lots of folks did. The device sold well over one million units. That's one million people who, after watching a commercial featuring a loser using a loud-speaker to accost women, thought "That's for me!" and bolted for the store.

When customers got the item home and unboxed it, they learned they'd purchased, well, an audio weapon. Yell into Mr. Microphone and your words instantly blared from the nearest properly tuned radio. Not until the invention of e-mail would the average Joe find a more effective way to force his personality and opinions on the unsuspecting (and usually unappreciative) masses. If you took the famous commercial seriously, then in theory no one was safe from Mr. Microphone. In addition to the idiot who used it to troll for babes, viewers also saw happy customers walking and even skating with the device, providing their own personal play-by-play coverage as they went.

This particular public broadcasting craze burned brightly but briefly. By the mid-'80s, the scourge of the ASOTV trade—the appearance of even cheaper knockoffs—had pulled the plug on Mr. Microphone. Radio Shack and other companies offered clones, and Popeil lost a court battle to stop them. But like nuclear weapons, once this particular technology escaped its bottle, nothing could stuff it back in. After all, what's a karaoke system but a sophisticated, overpriced Mr. Microphone?

Origins

Ron Popeil got the idea after watching a singer cavorting on TV with a wireless mic. Feeling it undemocratic to restrict such an entertainment breakthrough merely to the talented, he formulated a similar device that was soon available at area Woolworth's for $14.88. Another inventor had come up with the same scheme earlier, but with the help of engineers, a Hong Kong electronics firm, and a gaggle of lawyers, Popeil turned his version into a marketing legend.

Radio Bart

In a classic episode of *The Simpsons*, Homer orders a Mr. Microphone–like product for Bart's birthday. Soon Bart discovers he can use it to torment his parents, extort cookies by pretending to be God, and trick the town into believing he's a boy stuck in a well. In other words, all the standard second-week uses of a real Mr. Microphone.

Trivia Fact

The rock band Guided by Voices has used Mr. Microphone in its act.

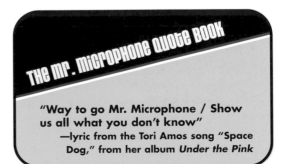

THE MR. MICROPHONE QUOTE BOOK

"Way to go Mr. Microphone / Show us all what you don't know"
—lyric from the Tori Amos song "Space Dog," from her album *Under the Pink*

POCKET FISHERMAN

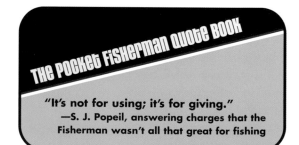

"Want to make a boy happy? Give him the Pocket Fisherman."

Average consumers—especially those over the age of 40—are usually flabbergasted to learn that the Pocket Fisherman is still for sale. Most assume it long ago went the way of other Golden Age Ronco gadgets such as the Veg-O-Matic (see page 12). But while those doo-dads languish in that great garage sale in the sky, the trusty Fisherman keeps luring new customers.

The package is so brilliantly self-contained it looks like something James Bond would carry—if James Bond would ever be caught dead fishing. The chief dig against the Pocket Fisherman is that it's hard, with a rod that's only about a foot long, to cast the line effectively. In this case, size does matter. And speaking of size, don't bring one to a bass fishing tournament. That's akin to showing up at a Harley-Davidson rally on a moped.

But those drawbacks pale before the Pocket Fisherman's advantages. The sheer novelty of being

---

THE PRODUCT

An all-in-one rod, reel, and tackle set that fits in a standard glove compartment.

STATUS: On the market.

CLAIMED INNOVATION: Fish anywhere, anytime.

THE UPSIDE: You can really fish with it.

THE DOWNSIDE: Does anyone besides Huckleberry Finn really need the ability to fish anywhere, anytime?

THE POCKET FISHERMAN QUOTE BOOK

"It's not for using; it's for giving."
—S. J. Popeil, answering charges that the Fisherman wasn't all that great for fishing

able to whip fishing tackle out of a glove compartment powered sales into the millions. In his book *Salesman of the Century*, Ron Popeil says the overwhelming success of the item forced him to look beyond his usual stomping ground, the kitchen, for inspiration. His newfound respect for the outdoor market was one of the reasons he trotted out a food dehydrator. It was something for all those jerky chompin', trail mix guzzlin' outdoor types to play with after a hard day on the lake with their Pocket Fisherman.

Like Father, Like Son

The fact that the Pocket Fisherman still finds buyers is silent testament to the skills of its creator, S. J. Popeil—father of Ron Popeil. Both the elder and younger Popeil focused their inventing prowess on the kitchen. But one day, an associate suggested to S. J. that he make something for the outdoor market. Although he wasn't much of an outdoorsman, and no kind of fisherman, for some reason S. J. and a team of engineers decided to design a fishing pole. A Gary Coleman–sized fishing pole.

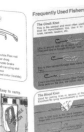

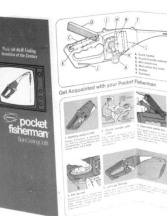

Unauthorized Use

Substitute a catnip toy for the lure and go "fishing for felines" in your own home.

Bizarre Product Endorsement

Ron Popeil named his boat the *Pocket Fisherman*.

Time-Life BOOKS

"You'll receive a new volume every month..."

The old West. World War II. Cooking. Is it ever possible to read too much about such fascinating subjects? The folks at Time-Life Books didn't seem to think so. In 1961 the company, a division of Time, Inc., started assembling mammoth, multivolume "themed" collections that exhaustively covered everything from combat to home repair. Then it hawked them on TV and sold them by direct mail. In time, these shelf-snapping monstrosities grew so popular that no middle-class rec room seemed complete without at least one collection monopolizing two or three feet of bookcase space.

The various series were monuments to the concept of delayed gratification. Most of them arrived at your home one piece at a time. The TV pitch ran something like this: "Each month you'll receive another volume of *Great Barbers of the Middle Ages*. If you like the book, keep it and we'll bill you. If not completely satisfied, return it and pay nothing." That seems like a pretty sound sales model, until you consider that someone who ordered the 39-volume Time-Life World War II series during, say, the last days of the Carter presidency might still be getting installments well into the Reagan revolution.

THE PRODUCT

Mail-order history and self-help books.

STATUS: Off the market.

CLAIMED INNOVATION: Learn all about some obtuse field of human endeavor for only (insert uncomfortably huge number here) monthly payments of $10.99.

THE UPSIDE: Fun to read, neat photography and illustrations.

THE DOWNSIDE: How much do you really need to know about the wild west?

THE DEATH OF TIME-LIFE BOOKS

When Time, Inc. (which had already merged with Warner Bros.) was swallowed by AOL to form AOL Time Warner, the media behemoth decided mail order books were no longer worth the bother. The division, which had endured declining sales for years, was eliminated in 2000. But its stablemate, Time-Life Music, still thrives.

If collecting the books required a long attention span, actually reading them didn't. Each was chock-full of photos and laden with subhead- and sidebar-intensive text, and individual editions rarely exceeded 200 pages. Think of them as the *USA Today* of textbooks. With the knowledge chopped into bite-size bits, the books made excellent bathroom literature. Perhaps that's why they got so little respect. If reading real books was like getting a Harvard Education, then purchasing a Time-Life series was the equivalent (in the eyes of critics) of a two-year community college degree.

Which, in retrospect, isn't at all fair. Examine the fine print in the backs of various volumes and you'll find that most were composed by recognized experts in their fields—even the stuff about Atlantis in the goofy *Mystic Places* series. As for the photos, many were rarely seen, important images. Many were even cribbed from the archives of *Life* magazine, which has been known to feature some interesting snapshots.

THE TIME-LIFE QUOTE BOOK

"Did you get that from a Time-Life Book?"
—Sarah Michelle Geller questioning someone's insight on the occult during a *Buffy the Vampire Slayer* episode

POP QUESTION

ARE THESE VINTAGE BOOKS WORTH ANY MONEY TODAY?

Surprisingly, yes. If you have a complete set in good condition you can probably sell it for near or even more than the original face value, depending on the subject. Complete sets are usually worth more because they're comparatively rare. Customers either lost interest before they received every volume or else Junior broke them up in 1977 when he spilled grape juice on *Russia Besieged*, the sixth volume in the 39-volume epic World War II series.

THE AS SEEN ON TV PARODY SHOWCASE
HERE'S OUR TOP 5

Infomercials and ASOTV products seem like fertile ground for satire, yet few humorists have skewered them well. Maybe it's because the real spots skate so close to parody that they defy all but the most seasoned comedy writers. Nevertheless, on a few memorable occasions the humor's been right on target.

5

THE MIKE TYSON GRILL

If George Foreman can make a fortune in the grilling business, why not Mike Tyson? Such was the simple-but-brilliant premise that sparked this *Mad TV* sketch. There are, of course, a few differences between Foreman's kitchen gadget and Tyson's. Specifically, while the former stresses fat-reduced cooking of burgers and chicken, Tyson (played by Aries Spears) promises "to revolutionize the way you fry bologna." Foreman is fairly articulate about the advantages of his appliance. Tyson mispronounces his way through the sales pitch and needs the assistance of, in a stroke of obscure-reference brilliance, Jenilee Harrison (Mo Collins). For those of you who don't remember, Harrison played Chrissy's cousin on *Three's Company* after Suzanne Somers left the show.

4

THRILLING MIRACLES

Fabu-Leg (a prosthetic), Buddy Board (basically, a seesaw), and Miracle Powder (cocaine) all were products featured on the faux infomercial *Thrilling Miracles*—or so said the opening sequence of this sketch from the demented geniuses behind the HBO comedy series *Mr. Show*. But those creations are just warm-ups for the introduction of Superpan, "developed by astronauts who quit the space program to devote their lives to developing pans." Featuring high-fiving host Pat Franks (David Cross); Ernie, the excitable pitchman from across the ocean (Bob Odinkirk); and perpetually astonished hostess Jill (Nancy Gumfrey), the sketch starts as a dead-on imitation of demonstration infomercials. However, it quickly devolves into an exercise in brutality. "I've got a Superpan that has been heating up on the stove for over nine hours," says Ernie to the crowd. "Do you want to see her [the female cohost] touch it?" After the inevitable scream of pain, Ernie tells the now wow-less Jill that she shouldn't listen to crowds. "The Superpan is not magical," he says. "It will burn you."

PITCHMAN TROY MCCLURE

If it weren't for the fact that he's fictitious, Troy McClure from *The Simpsons* (star of such films as *Preacher with a Shovel, Look Who's Still Oinking,* and *Calling All Quakers*) would certainly be in line for an infomercial lifetime achievement award. After all, the animated genius who fronts the program *I Can't Believe They Invented It!* has introduced to the world such products as The Juice Loosener, the beer-flavored gum Brew 'n' Chew, and Styro-Glow! (the 17-step solution to making Styrofoam look new). And that's not all. McClure, voiced by the late Phil Hartman, can also take credit for the Candy Bar That Cleans Teeth, Eyeball Whitener, and The Carbolanator (featuring 87 hard-to-use tools in one). No wonder Homer loves watching TV.

GORDON LIGHTFOOT SINGS EVERY SONG EVER WRITTEN

The best sketches from *SCTV* were multilayered affairs. For this one—an ad for what has to be the largest set of CDs ever offered on TV—it helped to have a good grasp of musical history, since Lightfoot had recorded it all. Our favorites: "Good King Wenceslas" and "76 Trombones." Harvey K-Tel, the spot's fast-talking announcer (Dave Thomas), vocally appeared in other episodes as well, plugging such discs as The D'Annamora Prison Choir's *For Lifers Only* collection and *5 Neat Guys Gold* (featuring "Mom Pressed the Crease in My Chinos"). He also served as front man for the Ricardo Montalban School of Fine Acting. Perhaps his oddest moment came as host of K-Tel's Fast-Talking Playhouse, featuring an announcer-paced version of *Who's Afraid of Virginia Woolf?*

BASS-O-MATIC

Of the original *Saturday Night Live* crew, Dan Aykroyd was the least human and the least charming (even less than Chevy Chase, which is saying something). Yet he was a genius when it came to single-minded characters who could look you right in the eye and lie. Such was the case with this first season *SNL* sketch in which Aykroyd relentlessly touted the virtues of Rovco's "amazing new kitchen tool," Super Bass-O-Matic '76. "Yes, fish-eaters," says Aykroyd, "the days of troublesome scaling, cutting, and gutting are over." He then demonstrates what happens when you put a whole bass in a blender. Of course, it wouldn't be Ronco, er, Rovco if there weren't a litany of items included. Here, that means 10 interchangeable rotors, a nine-month guarantee, and the booklet *One Thousand and One Ways to Harness Bass.* While Aykroyd gets most of the credit for the spot (and he should, since he wrote and performed it), attention must be paid to fellow cast member Laraine Newman, who, in a brief insert, downed a glassful of, presumably, pureed fish and exclaimed the immortal line, "Wow! That's terrific bass!"

part 5

Home Improvement
Miracles

Tired of looking at that annoying stain on the couch? Then it's infomercials to the rescue! Whatever the problem, there's a TV product that can steam, patch, or soak it away.

Garden Weasel

"Weasel your way out of yard work."

For decades, purchasers of this ultimate lawn care doodad have done double takes when they noticed on the packaging the name of the firm that offered it: the Faultless Starch/Bon Ami Company. That's right, the same folks who help us stiffen dress shirts and clean kitchen sinks also hawk one of the most peculiar-looking devices in the annals of tillage. It's as if Hershey marketed power sanders or Victoria's Secret trotted out a line of car batteries.

The curious relationship began in 1976 when Faultless chairman and CEO Gordon Beaham visited a lawn and garden show in Cologne, Germany. There he spotted an odd-looking contraption with three sets of interlocking spoked wheels that, when attached either to a long handle or a shorter pistol grip, churned up tilled soil. Beaham thought he'd spotted a winner and signed up to become the Weasel's North American distributor.

"Next thing you know they were bringing over a boatload or two of these things," recalls Webster "Web" Thompson, a then-new Faultless employee who, to his own surprise and chagrin, became the gadget's distributor. "My more senior associates at the time thought, 'What on earth have we done?'"

THE PRODUCT

A soil aeration tool that uses three sets of interlocking spoked metal wheels to churn dirt.

STATUS: On the market.

CLAIMED INNOVATION: Allows soil to be cultivated quickly and effortlessly.

THE UPSIDE: Works like a charm on loose, already-prepared beds.

THE DOWNSIDE: Useless on densely packed ground. You'd have better luck chopping down a tree with a butter knife.

THE GARDEN WEASEL QUOTE BOOK

"Your lawn also needs the Weasel. It provides it with the air to breathe."
—Garden Weasel box

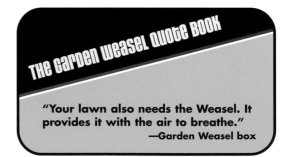

The folks on his sales route probably thought the same thing. At the time, Thompson was attempting to expand Faultless's market base by trying, not very successfully, to interest hardware distributors in the company's products. As if that weren't tough enough, now at the end of sales pitches he also had to whip out his Weasel. Few were impressed.

But then came Joseph Pedott, president of Joseph Enterprises and the marketing brains behind such megasellers as The Clapper and Chia Pets (see pages 90 and 88, respectively). Faultless called him in to help Thompson (who reverently refers to Pedott as "my mentor") soup up the Weasel's promotional program.

His immortal advice? Get the product into drugstores, then buy TV ads in local markets that encourage Joe Consumer to "weasel your way out of yard work." Thus began the Weasel's rocket ride to fame. Thompson isn't exactly sure when the homely device morphed from a mere product into a cultural icon. All he knows is that suddenly Johnny Carson was making fun of it on *The Tonight Show* and *Saturday Night Live* was using it in a sketch. But most importantly, Weasels started selling as fast as Faultless could import them.

wacky foreign names for the garden weasel

In Italy they call it *La Donnola del Giardino*. In France it's *La Belette de Jardin*.

unauthorized use

Freak out Hogarth and the rest of the gang by wielding it as a weapon at the next Renaissance fair.

pop goes the weasel

The Weasel's salad days ended in the late '80s when its patent protection ran out and the clones swarmed in. When the distinctive commercials vanished, the sales figures withered faster than an uprooted dandelion. As for the Weasel itself, it's still available from Faultless in the U.S. (and in so many other countries that the instruction manual is printed in nine languages).

To Webster Thompson the Weasel isn't just another cheap hoe. In fact, when he waxes poetic about the contraption it's hard to tell if he's talking about a garden tool or Che Guevara. "It's still remarkably and wonderfully alive in the minds of the people," he says.

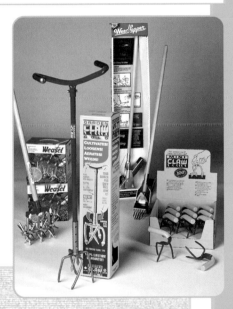

spin-offs

The Garden Claw, a four-pronged device surmounted by what looks like the steering yoke from an airplane. Stick the prongs in the ground, turn the yoke to the left and it can break up soil as efficiently as a hoe. Well, maybe not quite as efficiently, but with a lot less back pain.

Liquid Leather

"Don't throw away that expensive leather!"

Products similar to Liquid Leather have been around for decades, but none features a commercial that opens with quite as big a bang. Actually, it's not so much a bang as a stab. Viewers first see a tacky, *Miami Vice*-ish leather couch. Then, suddenly, a male hand plunges a knife deep into its teal-colored cushiness. Ordinarily there would be only two ways to deal with such an outrage: either duct tape the hole or cart the entire piece to the dump. But not with Liquid Leather. All you need is a little dab and a little heat to have that sofa looking good as new. Hopefully.

Here's how it works. The liquid leather isn't leather at all, but a urethane compound that solidifies into leatherlike pliancy when heated. To patch tears simply spread it, peanut butter–style, over the afflicted area. Then use a piece of "grain paper" that impresses a pattern into the urethane similar to that of the stricken spot, and apply heat for two minutes. Remove the paper and you have a perfectly matched, indistinguishable repair.

And that's all there is to it—except for one fateful step that's been the undoing of generations of amateur upholsterers. Since leather and vinyl products come in

UNAUTHORIZED USE

S & M party getting a bit rough? Liquid Leather can fix that busted bustier!

many colors, the Liquid Leather kit includes 10 "Intermix" shades that customers can combine to produce a matching tone. Problem is, if you don't produce a tone that exactly matches, you'll be looking at a slightly off-color patch on your jacket/car/couch for years to come. "But consumers can get pretty close, and for them that's very satisfactory," says Liquid Leather inventor Larry Speer. Especially since the alternative is to break out the duct tape.

INDUSTRIAL APPLICATIONS

A version of Liquid Leather is used by automobile factories to patch minor upholstery damage sustained during manufacturing.

SURPRISE BONUS USE

Don't throw out that damaged Elvis portrait or bullfighting scene! Liquid Leather comes with a free fabric mender kit that fixes velour!

THE AMAZING ORIGIN

Liquid Leather (originally called Minute Mender) was created by Larry Speer in the early '60s while running a small New York City refinishing shop. One of his biggest contracts was for the upkeep of a chain of Automats. "They had tons of vinyl seating and every time one got ripped we had to put a new seat cover on," Speer recalls. "The owner said, 'Isn't there any way to repair them so when there's a little rip it doesn't get any bigger?'"

Actually there wasn't—until Speer invented one. Intrigued by the problem, he visited a vinyl manufacturing facility to see how the product was made. His Liquid Leather uses a scaled-down variation of that process.

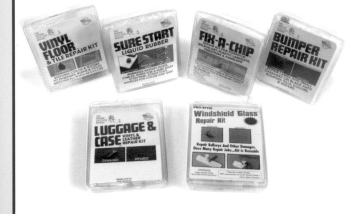

OxiClean and Orange Clean

"Powered by the air you breathe."

OxiClean debuted around 1995, but the fun didn't really start until a couple of years later when it landed a spot on the Home Shopping Network. Like the Jackson 5 at their first Apollo Theater appearance, OxiClean stood out. On live TV the crystalline compound (which is activated when mixed in warm water) destroyed stains in everything from rugs to dresses with wonderfully telegenic speed and finality. The product sold as never before. "After that," says Joel Appel, president of the company, "we decided we really needed to control our own destiny and make some infomercials."

Hosting duties fell to veteran pitchman Billy Mays, a great, bearded bear of a man who gesticulates furiously during the half-hour spots, praising the products in a loud, urgent tone reminiscent of the Crocodile Hunter, except he doesn't say "mate" every 10 seconds. Instead he incessantly repeats OxiClean's motto: "It's the cleaner that works so you don't have to."

During most of the productions (there have been about 10 so far) Mays runs around what looks like the interior of the Brady Bunch house like an eight-year-old on a Skittles high, dousing gravy, red wine, and other nox-

THE PRODUCTS

OxiClean is a powdered, shelf-stable hydrogen peroxide compound that's activated by mixing in warm water. Orange Clean harnesses the grease-cutting power of concentrated orange extract.

STATUS: On the market.

CLAIMED INNOVATION: Lifts out stains without the use of harsh chemicals.

THE UPSIDE: OxiClean really does blast away most nongreasey organic stains.

THE DOWNSIDE: It will also blast away noncolor-fast dyes, so be careful with that squirt bottle.

NOT-SO-FUN FACT

Hydrogen peroxide, highly diluted for use in OxiClean, makes a great disinfectant and cleaning agent. In its *undiluted* form it's strong enough to eat through human flesh and so volatile it can be used as a component in rocket fuel.

ious substances on every available surface. Then he cleans up the ensuing mess with either Orange Clean (a degreaser famous in its own right) or OxiClean (which cuts almost any organic-based stain).

Orange Clean gets its share of screen time, but it definitely plays Robin to OxiClean's Batman. Again and again Mays states that the tiny crystals are "Powered by the air we breathe and activated by the water that you and I drink." Then he dumps a cupful into warm water, puts the resulting solution into a squirt bottle, and attacks aluminum siding, jewelry, a wedding dress, a dirty board, even dentures.

Is it any wonder that customers praise it with words normally reserved for war heroes and Olympic athletes? Appel says lots of clients write about how OxiClean saved the day after they spilled red wine on white carpets. "We have letters about people's communion dresses that they spilled wine on 25 years ago," he adds. "They were finally able to get them clean so their granddaughters could wear them."

Hmmm. OxiClean is a great cleaning product, but maybe we're approaching the problem from the wrong perspective. It sounds as if people wouldn't need to reach for the cleaning solution so often if they were just more careful with the vino. As Mays himself states during a remarkably prescient infomercial moment, "Red wine is a nightmare."

mr. clean

In a field filled with marketing gurus who make fortunes from the inventions of others, the ASOTV story of Max Appel (father of president Joel Appel) offers a refreshing change. The saga of the Colorado-based inventor of Orange Clean and OxiClean began more than 15 years ago when the professional salesman hawked various products and contraptions at fairs and home shows. He became interested in home cleaning products primarily because they're perishable—customers would have to constantly buy more.

Appel found just what he wanted in a powerful industrial cleanser made by a Denver janitorial supply company. "He started bottling it and selling it at fairs," says Max's son, Joel. "Then he decided he wanted to come up with a better, more environmentally safe product, so he reformulated and started his own business."

Roto Zip Solaris

"Plunge, cut, and create."

Women made great strides in the twentieth century. They won the right to vote. They fought for equal pay for equal work. They even landed their mugs on two U.S. coins (although nobody uses either of them). But throughout the revolution, one bastion of male dominance stood tall—the chauvinistic world of power tools.

Almost everyone who wielded such implements, from Bob Vila to serial killers, was a guy. But all that changed in August of 2000 when Wisconsin-based Roto Zip Tool Corporation marketed a distaff edition of its oh-so-macho Roto Zip Spiral Saw. This particular version was the first such device specifically designed to be wielded by women, and it did for home improvement what Virginia Slims did for cancer sticks. Overnight the boys' club of power tools went the way of the Little Rascals' He-Man Woman Haters Club.

Going by the name Solaris, it was introduced at the National Hardware Show and Building Projects Exhibition in Chicago and trumpeted on infomercials and QVC. Basically a sawlike device that uses a revolving bit instead of the standard jagged teeth, it packs quite a punch into its two-pound casing. Promotional materials implied that now even a girl, if she used Solaris properly, could make garden

THE PRODUCT

A compact power saw.

STATUS: On the market.

CLAIMED INNOVATION: "The first power tool built specifically for women."

THE UPSIDE: Attractively designed.

THE DOWNSIDE: Probably not up to major home improvement projects.

ornaments, create bathroom tile designs, or craft a play table for the kids. One can only imagine what Lorena Bobbit could have done with it.

Are women really pushing to make birdhouses and tie racks? Bob Kopras, CEO and founder of Roto Zip, thinks they are. "The development of the Solaris is in direct response to the passing of the tool belt," he says. "*KIY Retailing Magazine* reports that females in dual income households initiate about 80 percent of all home improvement projects."

If by "initiate" he means that the wife says, "Honey, when the hell are you going to fix that fence?" he'll get no argument from us.

And the Winner Is . . .

Let other companies boast of snagging Infomercial of the Year for Best Female Spokesperson. At the 2001 awards presentation in Las Vegas, Roto Zip Solaris took home the coveted Product of the Year title, meaning that voters actually believe it works.

The Roto Zip Quote Book

"Women have shattered the wood ceiling when it comes to home repairs, and we've got the tool to fix it."
—Roto Zip founder and CEO Bob Kopras to United Press International

Steam Buggy

"You are giving your entire house a steam bath."

Infomercials always take the products they push way too seriously, but few go quite as far as one 30-minute pitch created for the Steam Buggy. In an opening sequence that rivals the intensity of the first 20 minutes of *Saving Private Ryan*, a harassed housewife struggles to scrub a grime-encrusted stove. Then it cuts to a shot of another woman wearing a gas mask as she attempts to clean a toilet using enough chemicals to fill a toxic waste dump.

Suddenly, like Dorothy opening the door to Oz, the infomercial sweeps us into the wonderful (and very, very sanitary) world of The Steam Buggy. Our hosts for this journey are, instead of Munchkins, the only-slightly-less-cuddly sales team of Terry Toner and Ken LuVaun.

The device they tout is a smallish yellow contraption about the size of a portable vacuum cleaner. But while vacuums suck, the Buggy blows. The machine, as the name implies, shoots out a jet of boiling hot steam. In the past, this heavy-duty janitorial technology only fell into the hands of civilians when they rented a steam cleaner from their local U-Haul. But now, for a couple of low payments, you can own the

THE PRODUCT

A portable steam cleaning unit.

STATUS: On the market.

CLAIMED INNOVATION: Makes the power of steam available for home use.

THE UPSIDE: Really does blast the living crap out of stains.

THE DOWNSIDE: It takes its sweet time doing it. The nozzle is quite small: Your arms may be tired by the time you finish steaming the garage.

Caveat

Steam Buggy comes across as a fairly unsanitary sanitizer. All it does is blast the mess out of its hiding place, liquefy it, and leave it in a big, steaming pile. If you want to actually remove it, you'll need a rag. Also, the force of the steam does indeed power stuff out of cracks, but it can also, if you aren't careful, power stuff deeper *into* cracks.

"ultimate cleaning solution"—which is fairly amusing because the whole point is that no cleaning solutions are necessary. Rather than using chemicals, the Buggy gets things sparkly and sanitary using heat and pressure alone. Over the course of the infomercial it opens up a can of dirt-fighting whoopass on everything from commodes to lawn furniture to kitchen cutting boards, cleansing them all to surgical suite standards.

It can do this because steam kills almost all living tissue—something to keep in mind when you're waving the high-pressure nozzle around as a threat to family members about to walk on your newly cleaned carpets. Of course Terry and Ken never come out and say that you can give yourself a pretty good scald if you aren't careful, but they do state—endlessly—that you should let the unit sit for a few minutes before attempting to change the (presumably piping hot) attachments.

NASTY INFOMERCIAL MOMENT

During a bathroom demonstration cohost Terry Toner unleashes the Steam Buggy on a toilet that looks like it was ripped from the New York City Port Authority men's room. The Buggy's ability to roust hidden gunk out of crevices is shown in all its stomach-churning glory as a blast of steam first liquefies and then exposes what appears to be the residue of a hundred errant pee streams. Cohost Ken LuVaun utters a heartfelt "That's disgusting!" as Terry nonchalantly wipes up the mess with a cloth. How much was she paid for this?

Life's a Pitch— the Rise of the Home Shopping Channels

No look at the ASOTV phenomenon would be complete without considering the rise of the home shopping channels. While conventional infomercials must battle a sea of "regular programming," The Home Shopping Network and its rival, QVC, offer a mercantile version of MTV—all sales, all the time.

Fittingly, this redheaded stepchild of television and advertising was born by accident. It happened in 1977 when a struggling radio station in Clearwater, Florida, accepted 112 electric can openers in lieu of cash to cover a hardware store's advertising bill. Having only so many cans to open himself, station manager Lowell Paxson decided to market the appliances on the air for $9.95 a pop. When the entire stock flew out the door, he inaugurated a radio sales program called The Suncoast Bargaineer. In 1982 Paxson and WWQT's owner started a local TV sales show along the same lines, and in 1985 they took the concept national. Interestingly, during its first five hours on the air the fledgling network sold only $352 worth of merchandise.

Needless to say, business picked up. Today HSN ships more than 34 million items per year.

Not that it has the field to itself. Things got interesting when Joseph Segel (founder of The Franklin Mint, home of such direct-sales oddities as the *Star Trek* chess set) caught a few minutes of HSN programming and decided he could do better. In 1986 he proved it by launching QVC, which started life with only 25 employees. Everyone from execs to janitors helped answer phones if a particular product sold well. Today they needn't be so multifaceted. QVC employs more than 12,000 people worldwide and shipped some 76 million packages in 1999 alone.

SALES STRATEGIES

What allowed QVC to soar past HSN? Experts say HSN's original "hard sell" format got them in trouble. In the old days goods were introduced and explained. Then, in an elaboration of the old "supplies are limited, act now" ploy, the item was offered to viewers for just a few minutes. A counter on the screen even showed how many units allegedly remained in stock. QVC took a different tack, doing away with time limits and adopting a more laid-back, talk-show-like format. Today viewers can watch regularly scheduled programs peddling everything from jewelry to sports memorabilia. So what if some of the "hosts" sometimes have less personality than the robots at Disney's Hall of Presidents? The goods keep flying out the door.

WHAT IS THIS STUFF?

QVC and HSN items run the gamut from designer clothes to garden gadgets—kind of like if Sears was a TV show instead of a store. But while most are nice, conservative items, a few look like they were snatched from the Twilight Zone gift shop. Take the wide assortment of creepy dolls, some costing hundreds of dollars, hawked regularly on both channels. Some are so unnervingly realistic it looks as if a taxidermist ran amok in a nursery school. HSN even offers dolls custom-made to look like your child, along with matching clothing for the parent, the kid, and the toy. Coming soon: Matching straitjackets for carting everyone off to the loony bin.

STAR POWER

Lots of celebs are associated with the two channels. Home Shopping Network personalities include Suzanne Somers (peddling clothing and self-help products); Wolfgang Puck (kitchen doodads); Susan Lucci (jewelry and accessories); and Vicki Lawrence (cosmetics). At QVC Marie Osmond hawks Marie Osmond Collectibles (mostly creepy-looking dolls); Richard Simmons sells everything from videos to exercise gear; and Joan Rivers (who recently celebrated a decade with the network) peddles costume jewelry.

PERHAPS THE WORLD'S WORST TOURIST TRAP

Should stay-at-home consumers summon the gumption to peel themselves off their rec room couches, QVC actually offers a tour of its West Chester, Pennsylvania, facilities. The QVC Studio Tour begins, appropriately, with a look at the studios, then winds through a photo gallery of memorable on-air moments and a Hall of Records—a "museum-like" salute to top-selling QVC products. What would you pay for this incredible value? $20? $30? How about just $7.50 for adults and $5 for kids! And they throw in, at no extra charge, a trip through the gift shop, chock full of QVC Studio Park logo merchandise.

part 6

get rich
quick!

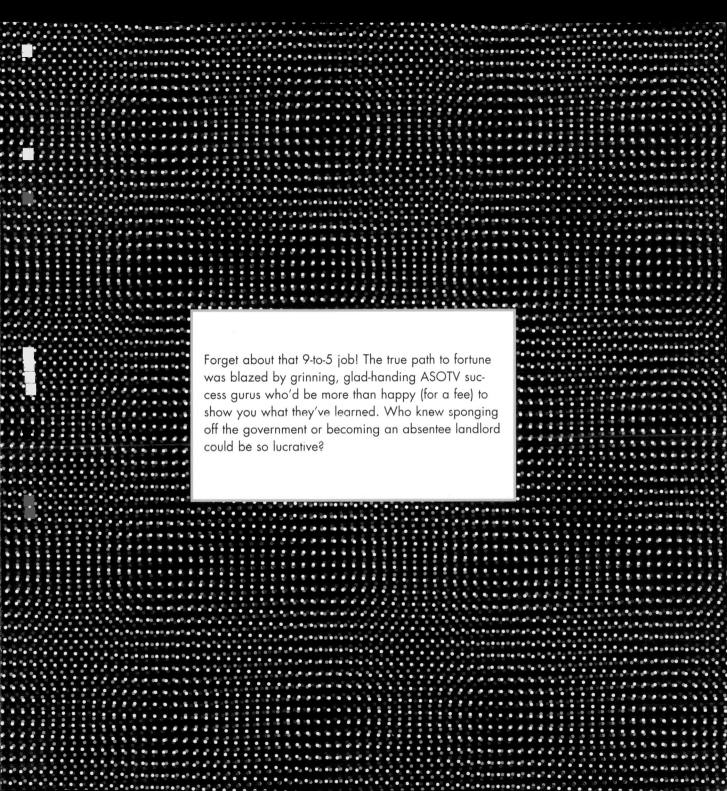

Forget about that 9-to-5 job! The true path to fortune was blazed by grinning, glad-handing ASOTV success gurus who'd be more than happy (for a fee) to show you what they've learned. Who knew sponging off the government or becoming an absentee landlord could be so lucrative?

DON LAPRE

"I guarantee that you will get excited!"

The world of retail is governed by a complex principle that the average person might find hard to grasp. But we're about to share it. Be sure not to drop this book, because when you read the next few lines you may gasp, involuntarily slap yourself on the forehead, and say, "Of course!"

Ready for the big secret? Here goes. In order to make money, you need to sell things for more than you paid for them.

Think you can handle a little more? Then wrap your mind around this: The less you buy something for and the more you sell it for, the bigger your profits.

Lesson one: Buy low, sell high. Lesson two: Buy lower, sell higher.

Got it? Good. Now you know just about everything that's on sides A and B of "Buying and Selling," part of a cassette series by financial guru Don Lapre, an open-collared, over-moussed guy who looks like the kid who loses his virginity early in an '80s movie starring Sylvia Kristel.

THE PRODUCT

Get-rich programs, most centered on selling items through classified ads.

STATUS: On the market.

CLAIMED INNOVATION: None. Just another version of the "get money while barely working" siren song.

THE UPSIDE: Easy-to-understand concepts.

THE DOWNSIDE: You're getting a pep talk from someone who seems no more financially savvy than Skippy from *Family Ties*.

THE CATCH

Laying down the $39.95 requested during Lapre's infomercial gets you a pack of books, tapes, and other peripherals. But the true sell comes later. That's when, according to people who've purchased the full program, Lapre's salespeople kick into high gear, pushing new converts to fork over even more cash for various Web- and 1-900-number–based programs. Hmmm. We guess *someone's* found a way to make money off of phone lines.

There are many paths to Rockefellerdom on Lapre's branch of the money tree. One is his aforementioned buying and selling concept (Alan Greenspan take note!). A second is to rake in the cash by starting a 1-900 number "business." A third is by selling goods through tiny classified ads. Quoth the Don: "Every time you place a classified ad in the newspaper, say to yourself, this ad could totally change my life if it makes me just $30 to $40 profit in a week . . . " Not since a fellow with the initials J. C. turned some loaves and fishes into a dinner party has such a stretching of resources been claimed.

But that's how you get rich in Lapre Land. During his *Making Money Secrets* infomercial he parades before viewers a cross section of humanity, all of them touting their success stories. There's the glowing elderly couple, the busty blond, and the guy who looks like David Lynch's Eraserhead. Each extols the virtues of Lapre's revolutionary plan. It certainly seems to have done well for its author, whose favorite hobby appears to be having his picture taken near large sums of cash. On the covers of his books, videos, and cassette kits he's shown being showered in bills. And on his official Web site he's buried up to his eyeballs in currency.

In truth his personal fortune would probably come no higher than his ankles. How else to explain the fact that this wealth-building genius filed for bankruptcy in 1999? Not that this ended his TV career. At press time he was still on the tube, teaching the Great Unwashed how to make a killing—although a standing-by operator stated Lapre is no longer with the company.

THE DON LAPRE QUOTE BOOK

"I hope and pray that Mr. Lapre burns in hell for his arrogance and callousness."
—Letter to the editor of the *Phoenix New Times* after a story ran discussing Lapre's bankruptcy

NOT ADDING UP

A publicity shot of Lapre shows him waving a bound stack of $20 bills. The wrapper on the bills says $250. So how is it possible for a bundle of $20s to add up to $250?

Matthew Lesko

"Has the U.S. government gone completely insane?"

It's hard to know how to feel after watching Matthew Lesko and his hyper TV spots. If you're looking for some quick bucks, you may love this guy. After all, the man cavorts around Washington, D.C., gleefully explaining how to shake down the government for fun and profit. Never mind that his suit is festooned with question marks (The Riddler must be fuming).

If you're a typical taxpayer who signs over a hefty chunk of his net worth to the IRS each April, though, you'll probably feel a little ill. That's because Lesko's main product is a phone book–size tome called *Free Money to Change Your Life*. It's a guide to roughly 15,000 government handout programs that are cumulatively worth some $350 billion. Much of the cash is earmarked for things such as student loans and business start-ups, but (as Lesko's own customer testimonials point out) the greenbacks also finance the most flagrant pork barrel giveaways. Lesko touts a couple who got $35,000 to start a hair salon; a guy who snagged $1 million in government grants to start a "consulting business"; and another who rounded up $500,000 to work on "his project" and travel overseas.

THE PRODUCT

A huge manual filled with enough government giveaways (along with tips on how to exploit them) to make Ronald Reagan puke.

STATUS: On the market.

CLAIMED INNOVATION: Lets Joe Public take advantage of little-known programs he's already helped pay for.

THE UPSIDE: Good, solid information.

THE DOWNSIDE: Seeing your tax dollars at work was never so depressing.

THE MAN

While many ASOTV "financial experts" are goofballs who strive to look serious, Lesko is a serious financial expert who strives to look goofy. A former consultant with a master's degree in computer science, Lesko spent years picking his way through the thickets of government regulations on behalf of his clients. Sensing an opportunity, he ditched his wonkish consulting gig, got a personality transplant, and became America's punctuation-bedecked guide to free government money.

The list goes on and on: $43,000 to become a French chef; $10,000 to put on poetry readings; and $5,000 to start a street hockey equipment business. Lesko doesn't take a David Horowitz–like consumer advocate stand on all this largesse. Instead, he points out that these programs will probably continue to exist whether we like them or not, so we might as well get our cut. As he states (again and again) in his promotional materials, firms such as Nike and Apple, along with individuals such as H. Ross Perot, weren't afraid to step up to the federal money tit. So why should we feel any differently?

THE MATTHEW LESKO QUOTE BOOK

"Our job is to let taxpayers know about these programs, whether they are fair or not. We all pay for them whether we use them or not."
—caveat on Lesko's Web site

SPIN-OFFS

Lesko has published some 70 books, including *Free Stuff for Pet Lovers*, *Gobs and Gobs of Free Stuff*, *Free Stuff for Seniors*, and *Free Health Care*.

ONE MORE HIDEOUSLY DEPRESSING TAX FACT

Lesko asserts that while 100 percent of families pay to support the programs he writes about, only 8 percent ever get money from them.

POP QUESTION

WHERE DOES HE GET THE GOOFY SUITS?

Lesko buys them off the rack, then has a seamstress sew on fabric question marks. At last report he owned five of them. He also drives a Lexus with yellow polka dots.

ANTHONY "TONY" ROBBINS

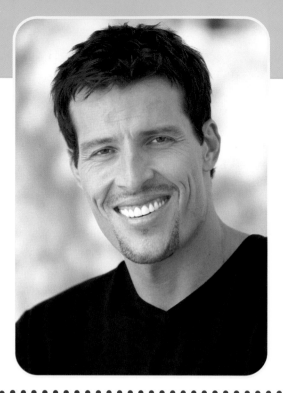

"Strategies for creating an extraordinary life."

Almost everything about Tony Robbins seems intimidating, from his physical stature (almost seven feet) to his self-help books with such Ayn Rand–like titles as *Unlimited Power* and *Giant Steps*. Even his infomercials are frighteningly out of scale. As his Web site proudly states, his half-hour spots have been airing around-the-clock since the first one was introduced in 1989. Which means he's always on the tube, somewhere.

Robbins needs all that airtime to sell a personal strategy that couples financial success with emotional development—a vinegar-and-oil mix that's hard for even the most enlightened mortals to manage. Robbins says he does it by, among other things, "modeling" the strategies of highly successful people, distilling them into easy-to-follow steps, and then spoon-feeding them to regular shmucks (our term, not his) through his seminars, books, and tapes. The most popular—and profitable—manifestation of this philosophy is the Personal Power audio series, which has sold some 25 million copies worldwide.

Robbins's doctrines are as oversized as the man himself. Words like "extraordinary" and "empowering"

THE PRODUCT

A huge array of tapes and books outlining Robbins' plan for personal success.

STATUS: On the market.

CLAIMED INNOVATION: Tips from the world's leading motivator.

THE UPSIDE: Lots of really successful people listen to him.

THE DOWNSIDE: It's tough to take seriously a guy who bears a disturbing resemblance to Richard Kiel (who played the James Bond villain known as Jaws).

crop up regularly. He's also a big fan of abbreviations and acronyms. "The 21st century educator must be an extraordinary Entertainer who Educates people with the finest tools, and Empowers them to act upon them. I call this philosophy, E3," he states. He also pushes something called Constant And Never-Ending Improvement, or CAN! We think that makes him a Really Immensely Creepy Hulk, or RICH.

Strangely, the folks who line up to hear this stuff aren't the typical sweatpants-wearing, 7-Eleven night-shift-working suckers who normally pack seminars. Robbins has spoken to *Fortune* 500 bosses and also counseled presidents and presidential contenders. Perhaps he's angling to become a twenty-first century Billy Graham—a secular sage earnestly telling the most powerful man in the world how to take his success to the next level. That's quite an advancement for someone who reportedly began his professional career as a school janitor.

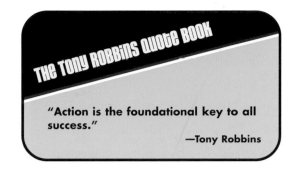

FASHION ALERT

For years Robbins dressed in suspendered suits and sported perfectly coifed hair and a 300-watt smile. He looked like the prototypical yuppie—or rather, some sort of *über* yuppie who was cloned in a CIA-operated tank farm. Lately though (perhaps because of his role in the Gwyneth Paltrow vehicle *Shallow Hal*) he's adopted a beard and artfully ruffled look. He's kind of like Johnny Depp—or rather, some sort of *über* Johnny Depp who was cloned in a CIA-operated tank farm.

SPIN-OFFS

The man has his huge fingers in lots of pies. One of the most scary-sounding is Mastery University, a "year-long educational experience" with instructors such as General Norman Schwarzkopf. Do students get extra credit if they overrun Poland?

Carleton Sheets
Real Estate Investment Training

"You don't have to have any money to buy real estate."

Let's get one thing straight. It is entirely possible to purchase real estate with very little money up front. It is also possible to become rich, even obscenely rich, doing so. But the people who succeed at this are usually smart, energetic, deeply experienced, and gifted with more killer instinct than an entire pack of wolves.

In other words, they aren't the sort of people who plunk down hundreds of dollars for the seminars and at-home courses peddled by ASOTV real estate guru Carleton Sheets.

His infomercials often air in predawn time slots, as if to catch harassed, overtaxed workers at their most vulnerable moment—when they first get up and realize they are facing one more day as losers. The spots, collectively called *The Carleton Sheets Program*, have been airing for almost 20 years. Over the decades their theme hasn't changed: how to get rich by buying real estate for no money down. According to his Web bio, Sheets, who became a full-time investor in 1970, learned the "creative financing techniques" necessary to do this by buying and selling more than $20 million in property.

THE PRODUCT

Tapes, CDs, and seminars preaching Carleton Sheets's "no down payment" guide to real estate investing.

STATUS: On the market.

CLAIMED INNOVATION: Increase your personal wealth with rental properties.

THE UPSIDE: We could all use a little education about the real estate market.

THE DOWNSIDE: Do you really think dream properties are that easy to come by?

THE CARLETON SHEETS QUOTE BOOK

"I don't have good credit and probably no chance to borrow money at a bank. How do I get around this?"
—actual FAQ query on carletonsheets.com

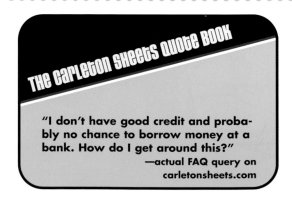

And now he wants to pass on those tips—for a not-so-nominal fee. His infomercials are come-ons for his enormous array of instructional tapes, books, CDs, and seminars. Sheets, who hammers relentlessly at the "no down payment" angle, also espouses the idea that becoming a landlord is fun and easy. His titles include *How to Skyrocket Your Profits Doing Quick and Easy Fix-Ups*; *How to Make Profits from Your Kitchen Table—World's Greatest Telephone Techniques*; and even *How to Get a Free College Education Using No Down Payment Investing*.

It's enough to make you fear for the future of the naive souls lining up for the seminars. Especially purchasers of the *Quick Start!* program that helps beginners move more rapidly into the thrill-a-minute world of real estate. If you're a novice at real estate investing, do you really want to plunge in as fast as possible?

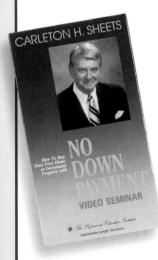

POP QUESTION

DOES THE SHEETS PROGRAM WORK?

Real estate investing builds wealth, and opportunities to buy no-money-down houses do occasionally arise. However, experts fault Sheets's program (which states that managing multiple properties takes only four or five hours a week) for making it sound easy. Sheets, intentionally or unintentionally, gives the impression that rental houses are low-maintenance money machines. Of course they aren't, as any rental property owner who's ever had to shake down tenants for last month's rent or fix an overflowing toilet at 2 A.M. can tell you. There's a reason why the landlords in movies and on TV are always grim-faced, grimy, and toting toolboxes.

SPIN-OFFS

The number and variety of Sheets's products boggles the mind. Some interesting non-lecture goodies include the *Real Profit$ Newsletter* (our unsolicited rule of thumb: Beware of anyone who uses a dollar sign in the place of the letter S) and the *Real Estate Computer ToolKit*—a CD loaded with property management software. Customers with lots of free time can purchase the No Down Payment Audio CD Course, which includes (among many, many other things) 12 CDs, almost 400 pages of course material, and numerous videocassette presentations.

INDEX

In the grand tradition of ASOTV pitchpeople, we couldn't resist making this book even more of a value by throwing in not two, not five, but 11 additional mini-entries celebrating even more of the products that make waiting for the mail so wonderful.

AUTO HAMMER

Hammering nails is easy. Just use one hand to hold the hammer, your other hand to pick up nails, and your third hand to position them. Okay, maybe it isn't so easy. To streamline the process, a company called Harvest Trading Group markets the handy dandy Auto Hammer. The device has a hollow handle into which nails are dropped. Shake the hammer headfirst toward the ground, and a nail from the reserve chamber falls out a hole near the head and is trapped in place by a magnet. Now just pound it into the surface in question and you're good to go. Sure, it takes practice to properly set nails (your first, second, and tenth tries will probably go sailing into the next room), but hey, that's the price of progress.

BACON MAGIC

You want a massive hit of artery-clogging fat but don't have time to fire up the stove? It's Bacon Magic to the rescue, offering the chance to cook as many as 10 strips of pork at a time—in the microwave. You achieve this feat of prestidigitation by draping the uncooked bacon over special cooking rods,

creating a sight oddly reminiscent of Salvador Dali's classic painting *The Persistence of Memory*, only with bacon instead of timepieces.

SLIM WHITMAN

Pop music is filled with "What the hell was that?" novelties. Tiny Tim. Alvin and the Chipmunks. Debbie Boone. But the oddest voice to achieve ASOTV fame was that of Slim Whitman, whose 1979 disc *All My Best* sold four million copies. With a three-octave range and a smile-inducing falsetto, the yodeling master serenaded fans and gag-gift buyers with "Love Song of the Waterfall," "Rose Marie," and, of course, "Una Paloma Blanca." The 6-foot-2 Florida native and former minor league baseball player was discovered by Col. Tom Parker, who introduced his sound to RCA Records. At one time his *Red River Valley* album held the No. 1 spot in England over the likes of ABBA and Queen. After roughly a decade out of the limelight, he reemerged thanks to help from the geniuses at Suffolk Marketing. Next time you're in Hollywood, look for his star on the Walk of Fame.

HOOKED ON PHONICS

Let other products address the improvement of abs, the elimination of excess body hair, and the shaping of the thighs. The folks at San Francisco–based Gateway Learning Corporation want to teach you and/or your child how to read. To do that, they combined games that no kid would ever play with books few kids would willingly read. The result is a national phenomenon. Disturbing fact: According to the company's disclosure information, Gateway has a trademark on the phrase ABCDEFG.

COPPER TONGUE SCRAPER

"Beat bad breath at the source in just a few seconds a day." So promised this device, the ASOTV contribution to the booming business of tongue cleaning. Apparently, brushing and flossing one's teeth aren't enough. True oral happiness can only come after you've plowed the bacteria off your tongue. This implement promised to reduce odors and bacteria by 75 percent. Add in another 10 percent from brushing and you've got, well, 85 percent less dragon breath. We like the illustration on the box, in which odors are made to seem visible and to rise, Chia Pet–like, from the chatty red muscle.

SHOWTIME ROTISSERIE OVEN AND BBQ

Ron Popeil made his name marketing simple, low-cost impulse items. But in the '90s he went big ticket, first with his food dehydrator and, more recently, with this kitchen-counter hog. On the infomercial, Popeil keeps a studio full of them going, striding from one to the next like an *Ed Sullivan Show* plate-spinner. To get a chicken cooking, he first impales the bird between a pair of round discs, creating what looks like a Wacky Racers poultry mobile. "All you have to do is set it," says Popeil, and his cultlike followers respond with, "and forget it." He boasts that the machine takes up no more shelf space than a toaster oven. Of course it's significantly more expensive than a toaster oven, but also a lot more interesting for an infant to stare at, meditatively watching the revolving chicken.

RONCO BOTTLE AND JAR CUTTER

Long before "reduce, reuse, recycle" became the mantra of suburban environmentalists, Ron Popeil was doing his part. The Ronco contribution to Mother Earth? This device, which turned discarded bottles and jars into glassware—albeit glassware that still looked a lot like discarded bottles and jars, only without the tops. A similar product already existed, but Popeil's innovation (and that of designer Herman Brickman) was to create a version that worked on square as well as round receptacles. The rest is hobby-graveyard history.

AS SEEN ON TV PC

We would be remiss if we didn't feature at least one product touted by veteran pitchman Mel Arthur. We could have gone with the ThunderStick Pro mixer ("replaces a kitchen full of appliances") or Sobakawa Magnetic Insoles. Instead, let us praise his work on behalf of the As Seen on TV PC. During this infomercial, Arthur takes the complex world of computers and brings it down to an ab-exerciser level. "It blows away anything you've seen in a Pentium III," he says of the processor. "We're going to give you memory," he goes on to boast, "not 128 megs of RAM. We're going to give you 256 megabytes of random access memory." When Arthur asks, "You want to talk about

peripherals?" we can only nod in agreement.

LITTERMAID SELF-CLEANING LITTER BOX

If we were dogs, we'd worry about future trends in pet ownership. One of the primary selling points for felines in the cats vs. dogs debate is that the former takes care of business in a litter box. With this innovation, that fact becomes an even greater plus. The folks at LitterMaid have come up with this remarkable device (which actually works). The cat triggers a sensor when it walks into the box. Ten minutes later (so as not to terrify the tabby), a raking cycle carries the clumped deposit into a sealed receptacle, which can then be removed. We want to write something funny here, but frankly we're still too awestruck.

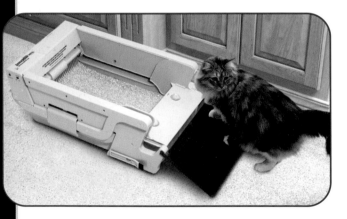

ZAMPHIR, MASTER OF THE PAN FLUTE

Apart from the centaur in the old Hercules cartoon, few pan-flute players have penetrated pop consciousness. That's why TV viewers couldn't help but stare when commercials appeared for a one-name wonder named Zamphir. Able to wrap his breathy instrument around everything from Rumanian folk songs to the theme from *Endless Love*, the Z Man recorded more than 130 discs besides the ones touted on TV. Trivia

fact No. 1: He does have a first name. It's Gheorghe. Trivia fact No. 2: Zamphir's music can be heard on the original soundtrack of the film *Once Upon a Time in America*.

CRAFTMATIC ADJUSTABLE BED

What better product to sell in the middle of the night than something for people who can't sleep? "You spend a third of your life in bed, why not spend it in a Craftmatic product?" these post-*Letterman* ads ask millions of exiles from the Land of Nod. Of course one could use the same logic to wonder, "You spend all of your life breathing, why not breathe in Barbados?" But that's really beside the point. The real point is that this firm has touted its line of adjustable beds on TV for more than a quarter of a century (or, in Craftmatic terms, more than 10,000 nights). "It's like taking your easy chair to bed with you," say company materials. In these spots, sleeping in a regular bed is made to sound like an overnighter in an iron maiden. Conventional bed owners are shown writhing in Dante-esque agony while Craftmatic sleepers lie happy as clams with their heads hiked higher than their butts—which are lower than their knees, which are higher than their feet (it is, after all, an adjustable bed). If Grandpa Joe in *Willy Wonka and the Chocolate Factory* had shared a Craftmatic Dual Super Extra Wide King, he never would have gotten up, golden ticket or no golden ticket. What's the appeal of a chocolate factory when you can fire up heat and massage options with the click of a remote control? Just add a bedpan, a refrigerator, and a widescreen TV and you could spend the rest of your life there.

ABOUT THE AUTHORS

Lou Harry's previous books include *It's Slinky* and *The Love Voodoo Kit*. The first album he ever bought was K-Tel's *Believe in Music*.

Sam Stall is the author of *Special Delivery*, the story of America's first sextuplets. As a child he wanted a Pocket Fisherman, but his parents didn't get him one. He never forgave them.

acknowledgments

We owe many thanks to David Borgenicht and Jason Rekulak at Quirk Books for making this project a reality, and to Cindy Harry, Mindy Kitei, Jami Stall, and John Thomas for reading, commenting, and correcting. Like the best infomercial phone operators, they were always standing by. Thanks to Steve Syatt and the Vegas crew for graciously granting access to the infomercial world. And a special thanks to Ron Popeil for talking.

144